ÉXITO DE SOLOPRENEUR

Tabla de Contenidos

Introducción 5
Capítulo 1: El ascenso del soloemprendedor 7
   ¿Qué es un solopreneur? 7
   Qué hace un solopreneur 9
   Lo que hace un emprendedor 9
   Solopreneurs y crecimiento profesional 10
   Cómo sabes que estás listo para ser un solopreneur 11
Capítulo 2: Crear un enfoque empresarial único 14
   Elegir su enfoque de negocio 15
   Cómo vender a un nicho de mercado 17
   Construyendo un Mercado 18
Capítulo 3: Trabaje más inteligentemente, no más difícil 20
   Cómo deshacerse de las distracciones 20
   Contratar un asistente virtual 21
   Externalizar y delegar trabajo 22
   Desarrolle sus habilidades de gestión del tiempo 23
   Utilice la tecnología 24
Capítulo 4: Mantenerse productivo 27
   Siga una rutina coherente 27
   Organice 28
   Establecimiento de objetivos 29
   Mantenerse productivo en casa 30
   Aprenda sus horas de productividad 31
   Pruebe primero una tarea pequeña 32
Capítulo 5: Red para el éxito 35

Construyendo su red 35

Conéctese a través de las redes sociales 36

Construyendo tu audiencia 37

Realizar investigaciones 38

Hacer que las redes sean divertidas 39

Capítulo 6: Saber cuándo pagar por las herramientas ... Y cuándo no 41

¿Es útil? 41

¿Con qué frecuencia lo usará? 42

¿Hay una versión gratuita? 42

¿Se ajustará a su presupuesto? 42

¿Se puede subcontratar? 43

Ejemplos de herramientas en línea 43

Capítulo 7: Concéntrese en el progreso, no en la perfección 46

Por qué no quieres perfeccionismo 46

La perfección es imposible 47

Cómo centrarse en el progreso 48

Cómo realizar un seguimiento de su progreso 48

Capítulo 8: No olvides tu tiempo libre 51

Cómo tomar descansos 51

Qué hacer en su descanso 52

Por qué necesitamos descansos de trabajo 53

¿Cuánto tiempo debe ser su descanso? 54

Aumentar la productividad 54

conclusión 57

Sobre el autor 58

legal 58

Sin responsabilidad 59

derechos de autor 59

Introducción

¿Estás interesado en iniciar tu propio negocio y convertirte en un emprendedor en solitario? Este ebook tiene todo lo que querrás saber. Como emprendedor en solitario, serás responsable de tu propia productividad, lo que puede ser difícil para muchas personas.

Usted tendrá que aprender disciplina, tener rutinas en su lugar, y trabajar en completar todas sus metas. Por supuesto, usted no necesita hacer todo este trabajo por su cuenta. Como propietario de un negocio, necesitará saber qué tareas necesitan su atención y cuáles subcontratar.

Además, también cubriremos el marketing de contenidos y las estrategias de negocios de redes sociales que puede usar para promover su marca. Hay mucho que cubrir. Si está considerando seriamente convertirse en un solopreneur, querrá leer nuestra guía: nos aseguraremos de repasar hasta los detalles más pequeños. ¡Empecemos!

The Rise of the Solopreneur

Capítulo 1: El ascenso del soloemprendedor

Si te gusta trabajar de forma independiente, entonces podrías ser el ajuste perfecto para un solopreneur. Muchos solopreneurs disfrutan trabajando solos y no quieren tener un jefe al que reportar. Es posible que incluso ya tenga algunas ideas en proceso para su negocio.

¿No estás seguro de lo que hace un solopreneur? Muchas personas confunden este título con "empresario"- si bien tienen muchas similitudes, también tienen algunas diferencias esenciales que usted querrá tener en cuenta.

¿Qué es un solopreneur?

Un solopreneur es un individuo que dirige su propio negocio. No requieren que ningún cofundador se inicie y no tienen ningún empleado W-2. El solopreneur se siente cómodo ejecutando todas sus tareas y proyectos de negocio. Esto requiere que tengan muchas habilidades en una amplia gama de temas.

Un solopreneur puede subcontratar parte de su trabajo a contratistas o freelancers. Sin embargo, no necesitan un W-2 de usted. Esto le permite seguir trabajando con profesionales para ayudar a construir su marca, sin tener empleados.

Un solopreneur puede caer en muchas industrias diferentes. Los siguientes son algunos ejemplos de un solopreneur:

- Diseñador gráfico o escritor independiente
    - Asistente virtual
    - Consultor de negocios
    - Propietario de una pequeña empresa
    - Gestor de redes sociales

Se espera que los trabajadores independientes reciban más oportunidades de carrera en los próximos años. Además, los registros indican que la mayoría de los solopreneurs se sienten más cómodos trabajando por su cuenta y lo prefieren sobre los trabajos tradicionales. Muchos también se sienten menos estresados con su trabajo y creen que es mucho mejor para su salud mental.

Si desea un trabajo que le proporcione un crecimiento y una satisfacción constantes, entonces una carrera de solopreneur podría ser una combinación perfecta para usted. Con una vida más flexible, usted puede construir su horario para adaptarse a usted el mejor.

Sin embargo, muchas personas confunden a los solopreneurs con los emprendedores. Es importante que conozcas la diferencia si quieres entrar en esta profesión. **Un solopreneur es el fundador y único empleado del negocio.** Un emprendedor generalmente tendrá un equipo que maneja. En general, los solopreneurs tienen mucha más libertad entre las dos posiciones.

Aquí, cubriremos las principales diferencias con más detalle a continuación.

Qué hace un solopreneur

Un solopreneur está a cargo de todos los aspectos de su marca y negocio. Por lo general, manejarán la mayoría de las tareas y proyectos de negocios por su cuenta. Si bien pueden subcontratar algunas tareas o contratar profesionales para ayudarlos con el trabajo que no pueden hacer, un solopreneur es el único empleado de su negocio.

Por ejemplo, un solopreneur puede contratar a un diseñador gráfico para ayudarles a construir y crear un sitio web. Este proceso no forma parte del día a día de la operación comercial de la marca, pero sigue siendo esencial para el crecimiento del negocio. Como emprendedor en solitario, no dudes en trabajar con profesionales freelancer cuando no puedas manejar la tarea por tu cuenta.

Además, el solopreneur es el fundador del negocio. Son responsables de crear todos sus productos o servicios y de hacerlos llegar a sus clientes.

Lo que hace un emprendedor

Si bien un empresario puede comenzar su negocio por su cuenta, por lo general no permanece así por mucho tiempo. Contratarán un equipo para manejar proyectos y tareas, principalmente creando los productos o servicios de la empresa. Los empleados también son responsables de garantizar que los clientes obtengan lo que pagan. En definitiva, un emprendedor delega más trabajo que el emprendedor en solitario.

Un emprendedor es más como un gerente. Dirigen su negocio supervisando el trabajo de las personas que contratan. Muchas personas se sienten más cómodas como un solopreneur, porque no están en una posición de gerente.

Solopreneurs y crecimiento profesional

A medida que construya su negocio, comenzará a notar más oportunidades que vienen en su camino. Una vez que tienes la pelota rodando, confía en nosotros, se vuelve más fácil. Ese "empujón" inicial puede ser muy difícil, pero pronto, tendrá la oportunidad de un montón de crecimiento profesional.

Este crecimiento profesional puede incluir:
- Mayores flujos de efectivo
- Alcanzar las metas de la carrera
- Aprender nuevas habilidades
- Ganando más experiencia

El crecimiento profesional es esencial para que cualquier emprendedor en solitario tenga éxito. Cuanto más aprendas, mejor podrás usar tus habilidades para mejorar tu negocio. Esto crea un ciclo positivo que le permite a usted y a su negocio seguir creciendo y mejorando juntos.

La mejor manera de crecer como solopreneur es desarrollar su red. Cuando más personas sean conscientes de ti, tendrás más oportunidades de construir relaciones comerciales con otros profesionales. Puede obtener más exposición, y más trabajo o ventas, a través de su red.

En general, dirigir su propio negocio pondrá a prueba sus talentos naturales. Trabajarás duro para desarrollarlos en habilidades profesionales, lo que te permitirá crecer más y obtener un ingreso constante.

Cómo sabes que estás listo para ser un solopreneur

Hay varias señales de que está listo para construir su propio negocio. Estos son algunos de ellos:

- Tienes una pasión
- Crees en tus talentos e ideas
- Tienes una idea de marca en su lugar
- Tiene un producto o servicio que ofrecer
- Estás listo para aprender y hacer un plan

Si bien hay muchas señales, la más importante es que te encanta aprender. Los solopreneurs necesitan ser un "gato de todos los oficios" - ya que manejan todo dentro de su negocio. Esto significa que usted tendrá que aprender un montón de habilidades y técnicas con el fin de tener éxito.

Por supuesto, todos los solopreneurs necesitan algo que les apasione. ¿Has escuchado el dicho "Si amas lo que haces, nunca trabajarás un día en tu vida", eso es cierto para los solopreneurs. Usted tendrá que invertir *mucho* de su tiempo en la gestión de su negocio. Sin embargo, esto va a ser lo que te haga crecer.

Además, cuando tu audiencia vea que amas tu carrera, estarán mucho más interesados en lo que tienes para ofrecerles.

Capítulo 2: Crear un enfoque empresarial único

El primer paso para comenzar su nuevo negocio es elegir un solo enfoque. Los solopreneurs generalmente comienzan atendiendo a un nicho de mercado, donde pueden construir una audiencia activa e interesada. Usted querrá tener una base de clientes estable antes de pasar a cualquier otra cosa.

Tener clientes confiables es esencial; mantienen su negocio rentable y le permiten interactuar con ellos fácilmente. Además, una sólida base de clientes mantiene su negocio fácil de administrar. Si empiezas a ramificar demasiado, es posible que tengas problemas para manejar todas las tareas por tu cuenta.

Su enfoque de negocio único tendrá que estar en el centro de todos sus servicios y productos. Por ejemplo, si estuviera dirigiendo un negocio de diseño gráfico independiente, se centraría en entregar los gráficos que sus clientes querían. Es probable que no se ramifique demasiado en otras áreas.

Esta es otra diferencia entre emprendedores y emprendedores en solitario. Un empresario que dirige un negocio de diseño gráfico tendría un equipo de diseñadores trabajando para ellos. Podrían ofrecer más servicios, lo que sería difícil para una sola persona.

Aún así, tu único enfoque debe ser lo que amas. Tener un servicio o producto principal también le permite atender a un nicho de mercado, donde hay menos competencia. Muchos trabajadores independientes pueden cumplir todos sus objetivos haciendo esto.

Por lo tanto, antes de que pueda comenzar a trabajar como solopreneur, necesita saber cómo vender a un nicho de mercado.

Elegir su enfoque de negocio

Tu enfoque empresarial va a ser el centro de todo lo que haces, no quieres elegir algo que puedas no gustarte o aburrirte más tarde. ¿Cuál es tu pasión? ¿Tienes algún pasatiempo que quieras comercializar? Si amas lo que haces, es mucho más probable que tengas éxito.

Siga estos pasos para determinar cuál debe ser el enfoque de su negocio:

- **Concéntrese en su pasión:** Si le apasiona el negocio, debe disfrutar de su gestión. También es más probable que tenga experiencia en su pasión o estará mucho más dispuesto a aprender sobre ella. Un montón de talentos pueden ser comercializables. Por ejemplo, estas son todas las habilidades que pueden ser comercializables:
    - Arte/Diseño
    - Escritura
    - Tejer y coser
    - Construcción de computadoras

- **Considere el equilibrio entre el trabajo y la vida personal:** Para muchas personas, equilibrar el tiempo que pasa trabajando es importante. Desea asegurarse de tener tiempo para sus pasatiempos, relajarse y pasar tiempo con sus seres queridos. Es posible que desee evitar la creación de un negocio que requiere largas horas de trabajo. Si bien puedes trabajar desde casa, eso no significa que quieras pasar todo tu tiempo "en el reloj".

- **Pon a prueba tu**enfoque: Antes de que el negocio funcione oficialmente, es importante que pruebes tu idea de enfoque. Usted querrá investigar:
    0   Demanda de su producto o servicio
    o   ¿Cuánto cuestan las startups y puedes permitírtelos?
    o   Qué puedes hacer para destacar de la competencia
    o   ¿Su producto o servicio resuelve los problemas de su audiencia?

- **Haga un plan:** A continuación, querrá escribir su plan de negocios. Esto debe incluir todos los pequeños detalles, así como sus grandes objetivos. Asegúrese de incluir cómo lograrlos. Escribir un plan completo asegura que hayas pensado en todo, lo que te da una oportunidad mucho mejor de lograr el éxito.

Si todavía tiene problemas para determinar cuál debe ser su enfoque de negocio, ¡está bien! Quieres pasar mucho tiempo pensando en tu enfoque; está bien esperar un poco para asegurarse de que tiene todo bien.

En resumen, su enfoque empresarial debe ser algo único que le guste hacer. Es difícil trabajar en campos que te aburren: perderías interés en el negocio rápidamente, y luego probablemente perderías tu inversión en la start up también.

Cómo vender a un nicho de mercado

Una vez que tenga su enfoque de negocio, tendrá que aprender a vender a ese nicho de mercado. Querrás saber todo lo que puedas sobre tu audiencia. A partir de ahí, puede utilizar su enfoque para crear su estrategia de marketing.

Una estrategia de marketing de contenidos bien pensada es esencial. Por suerte, usted puede construir su propio en línea. Muchos trabajadores independientes dirigen páginas de redes sociales para sus marcas. Para hacer esto, deberá trabajar en su identidad de marca y luego centrarse en cargar contenido consistente.

Su enfoque de negocio único puede conducir a una gran estrategia de marketing de contenidos de forma natural. Por ejemplo, si eres un fotógrafo que busca comercializarse a sí mismo, publicar tus fotos profesionales a menudo en Instagram sería extremadamente beneficioso para ti.

Si su negocio ofrece productos, entonces usted puede encontrar un montón de maneras de comercializar en línea. La publicidad en redes sociales es una excelente manera de atraer tráfico a su sitio web, lo que aumenta las ventas. Cuando se trata de audiencias de nicho, desea estar seguro de que sus anuncios son atractivos para ellos, de lo contrario, está desperdiciando sus fondos.

Lo más importante, tómese el tiempo para interactuar con su audiencia y escucharlos. Sus clientes saben lo que quieren y le dirán.

Construyendo un Mercado

¿Es su idea tan nicho que no hay un mercado obvio? Siempre puedes intentar hacer el tuyo propio. Para ello, tendrá que invertir mucho tiempo en su campaña de marketing. También te recomendamos que te centres en las cuentas de redes sociales de tu marca.

Una vez que haya encontrado a su audiencia, debe mostrarles por qué deben comprar sus productos o servicios. La mejor manera de hacer esto es crear una historia convincente en torno a su enfoque de negocio. Los clientes potenciales querrán ver todos los beneficios que su negocio tiene para ofrecerles, antes de realizar cualquier compra.

Puedes contar tu historia a través de la creación de contenido. Haz videos, imágenes y artículos. Asegúrese de incluir todos los beneficios que tiene su marca, así como lo que la hace diferente de sus competidores.

Work Smarter, Not Harder

Capítulo 3: Trabaje más inteligentemente, no más difícil

Una vez que su negocio esté en funcionamiento, deberá elegir qué tareas merecen su tiempo. Si te divides entre demasiadas tareas pequeñas, tus proyectos más grandes nunca van a recibir el tiempo que necesitan.

Una de las mejores maneras de hacer esto es mantener un planificador. Dentro de usted querrá registrar todas las cosas importantes que necesita hacer. Su lista de tareas pendientes debe incluir fechas y estar organizada por importancia, siempre maneje primero las tareas más esenciales.

Sin embargo, es posible que su negocio esté creciendo demasiado rápido para que pueda mantenerse al día. Ahí es cuando necesitas trabajar más inteligentemente, no más duro. Hay muchas maneras de hacerlo.

Cómo deshacerse de las distracciones

Primero, deshazte de las distracciones mientras trabajas. Todos somos culpables de revisar nuestros teléfonos celulares en el trabajo, pero esto puede ser muy perjudicial para la productividad. Esto es especialmente cierto para los solopreneurs, que no tienen un jefe que les diga que vuelvan a trabajar. Tendrás que asumir la responsabilidad por ti mismo.

Siempre silencia tu teléfono durante tus horas de trabajo. También hay muchas aplicaciones de administración del tiempo que es posible que desee considerar el uso. Dado que es probable que trabaje desde casa, tendrá que ser más disciplinado consigo mismo para completar el trabajo.

Al principio, puede ser difícil romper los malos hábitos telefónicos. Comience por silenciar su teléfono y dejarlo a un lado mientras trabaja en tareas esenciales, esto puede hacer una gran diferencia para muchas personas.

Contratar un asistente virtual

Un asistente virtual es alguien que puede ayudarte con pequeñas tareas de formaremota. Programarán reuniones y citas, harán llamadas telefónicas, manejarán correos electrónicos, y otras clases de tareas del planeamiento. Son muy parecidos a un asistente de oficina, aunque trabajan desde su casa.

Los asistentes virtuales pueden ser esenciales cuando tienes demasiado trabajo amontonado en tu plato. En lugar de responder a docenas de correos electrónicos usted mismo, el asistente lo hará por usted. De esa manera, puede poner todo su tiempo y enfoque en las tareas más grandes que ayudan a su negocio a crecer.

Es posible que se sorprenda de la cantidad de tiempo que pasa haciendo llamadas y respondiendo a los correos electrónicos. Una vez que obtenga esas tareas no esenciales de su camino, su negocio crecerá mucho más rápido.

Externalizar y delegar trabajo

A continuación, puede externalizar y delegar algunos proyectos a freelancers. **Si estás empezando a tener menos tiempo para administrar tus redes sociales, contrata a alguien para que lo haga por ti.** Los gerentes profesionales de redes sociales pueden mejorar su participación y publicar contenido según sea necesario. Notarás más crecimiento cuando un profesional te esté ayudando.

Puede contratar diseñadores para crear iconografía para su negocio, hacer que otra persona subtitule o traduzca su contenido de video, contratar a un escritor para hacer sus publicaciones de blog y más. Si tiene una tarea que consume demasiado tiempo o es demasiado difícil, hay profesionales en línea que quieren trabajar con usted.

La mejor parte, usted puede hacer toda la contratación en línea. UpWork, Freelancer, Fiverr, Indeed y Guru son solo algunos ejemplos de plataformas en línea. Estos sitios tienen toneladas de freelancers que buscan oportunidades de trabajo, seguramente encontrarás a alguien que ocupe los roles que tienes.

En general, es importante que los empresarios en solitario se sientan cómodos delegando o subcontratando su trabajo. A medida que su negocio crece, puede haber demasiados proyectos para que los administre todos a la vez. Al dividir el trabajo entre otros, se asegura de que tiene tiempo suficiente para completar sus tareas esenciales.

Desarrolle sus habilidades de gestión del tiempo

Por supuesto, cada solopreneur va a necesitar habilidades sólidas de gestión del tiempo. Aquí hay algunos consejos rápidos para desarrollar aún más sus habilidades de gestión del tiempo:

- Comience los proyectos temprano
- Priorizar tareas importantes
- Planifique con anticipación con frecuencia
- Hacer una lista de tareas diarias
- Tome descansos
- Programar y planificar en torno a los plazos
- Mantenga sus áreas de trabajo organizadas
- Haga un seguimiento de cuándo es más productivo
- Usar aplicaciones para establecer recordatorios y temporizadores

En su mayor parte, la gestión del tiempo requiere que te sientes y trabajes. Tendrá que reservar tiempo para ser productivo, pero esto todavía puede ser difícil para muchas personas. Nos gusta procrastinar, que puede ser un hábito difícil de romper.

Siempre comience a trabajar a la misma hora todos los días. Tome descansos constantes, luego termine sus horas de trabajo al mismo tiempo. Al seguir una rutina, su cerebro se animará a aumentar su productividad. Si usted no tiene una rutina, sería mejor planificar uno antes de convertirse en un solopreneur oficial.

Tomar descansos a menudo ayudará a mantener su mente fresca y lo alentará a ser más productivo. La Técnica Pomodoro es simple y fácil de seguir. Simplemente configure un temporizador para 25 minutos, trabaje todo ese tiempo y luego tómese un descanso de cinco minutos. Repetirás este proceso hasta que hayas terminado con el proyecto, ¡te sorprenderá la diferencia que esto puede hacer!

Utilice la tecnología

También puede externalizar algunos pequeños grupos de tareas mediante aplicaciones o inteligencia artificial. Por ejemplo, podrías usar un bot de redes sociales para responder a tus mensajes. Esto le dará más tiempo para trabajar en otros proyectos más grandes.

Las aplicaciones también son extremadamente útiles para cualquier solopreneur. Una aplicación de gestión del tiempo puede rastrear cómo está gastando su tiempo y ayudarlo a corregir sus hábitos donde sea necesario. Este proceso puede permitirle crear un flujo de trabajo más eficaz.

Las aplicaciones de gestión del tiempo le ayudan a mantener un buen equilibrio entre el trabajo y la vida personal. Te harán saber si estás trabajando demasiado duro e ignorando otros aspectos de tu vida, así como te alertarán si estás postergando tus proyectos. Estas aplicaciones también son ideales para determinar qué tareas ocupan más tiempo, lo que le permite determinar si está gastando su tiempo sabiamente.

En general, cada solopreneur tiene una amplia gama de tecnología disponible para ellos. Puede hacer uso de aplicaciones y ai para ayudar a externalizar su trabajo, así como revisar la forma en que está gastando su tiempo actualmente.

Staying Productive

Capítulo 4: Mantenerse productivo

Una vez que tenga todas sus herramientas de gestión del tiempo en su lugar, usted querrá mantenerse productivo. ¿Has escuchado "un objeto en reposo se queda en reposo y un objeto en movimiento permanece en movimiento"? Si bien esta es la famosa ley de física de Newton, también se puede aplicar a la motivación.

Cuando eres productivo es mucho más fácil seguir siendo productivo. Cuando no está completando tareas, se vuelve mucho más difícil comenzar de nuevo.

Hay muchas maneras en que puede mantenerse productivo. Si bien puede ser difícil al principio, continuar siendo productivo será más fácil con el tiempo. Esto es lo que querrá hacer.

Siga una rutina coherente

Tener una rutina consistente te va a beneficiar mucho, especialmente si estás trabajando desde casa. Su horario diario debe ser único para usted, pero aquí hay algunos consejos para que comience a construir su plan:

- Despierte a la misma hora todos los días
- No abras las redes sociales ni te conectes de inmediato
- Ejercicio y estiramiento, seguido de una ducha
- Desayuna y tu café de la mañana
- Establezca metas diarias y haga sus planes

- A trabajar
- Asegúrese de tomar descansos
- Terminar a la misma hora todos los días

Al seguir la misma rutina cada día, tendrás más fácil mantenerte productivo. Cuando comiences a seguir tus pasos, tu cerebro comenzará a entrar en "modo de trabajo" gradualmente. Este proceso le permite estar más enfocado, en lugar de simplemente lanzarse a su trabajo cuando sea.

Si desea ser un solopreneur a tiempo completo, entonces usted tendrá que tratar su horario en consecuencia. En resumen, la mejor manera de hacerlo es con una rutina consistente.

Organice

A continuación, querrás organizar todo en tu vida. Es mucho más fácil trabajar cuando estás rodeado de un ambiente limpio. Sin embargo, también querrá organizar sus planes. Hacer un montón de listas. Usted querrá trabajar en tareas esenciales primero, a continuación, trabajar su camino hasta los más pequeños.

Ayuda a utilizar su propio sistema de gestión de proyectos. Como emprendedor en solitario, desea administrar todos sus proyectos de manera efectiva. Hacerlo lo mantendrá en la tarea y también evitará que se olvide de los proyectos de diferentes clientes.

Su sistema siempre debe ser uno que está diseñado para la forma en que opera. Comience por construir una estructura que pueda seguir todos los días. Si no se siente como si estuviera funcionando, entonces no tenga miedo de cambiarlo. Después de todo, este es su plan. Necesitas hacer que funcione para ti mismo.

Si tienes demasiado que hacer para organizarte, un asistente virtual podrá ayudarte. Al liberar su tiempo, le permiten construir una estructura diaria más fuerte que funcionará para usted.

Establecimiento de objetivos

También es esencial que establezcas metas para ti y para los negocios. Una vez que complete un objetivo importante, será más fácil pasar al siguiente de inmediato: aumentar su productividad. Hay buenas maneras de establecer metas y maneras que usted querrá evitar.

Siempre debe establecer metas alcanzables. Si no puedes cumplir tus metas, te desanimarás. Eso puede conducir fácilmente a caídas en su productividad. Las metas alcanzables incluyen metas diarias, semanales y mensuales.

Para establecer un objetivo alcanzable, utilice el acrónimo SMART. Esto significa Específico, Medible, Alcanzable, Relevante y Período de tiempo.

Querrás que tus objetivos sean específicos. Por ejemplo, tener el objetivo diario de comenzar a trabajar a tiempo o ganar una cierta cantidad de ingresos en un día. Entonces, usted querrá comprobar adentro con sus metas semanales y así sucesivamente. Al establecer objetivos específicos, conocerá los estándares exactos para considerar el objetivo "completo".

Cuando somos vagos, puede ser difícil saber cuándo hemos terminado con una tarea.

A continuación, su objetivo debe ser medible. Decir "quiero ganar más ingresos este mes que el anterior", está bien, pero ¿cuánto más quieres ganar? Una mejor meta sería "Quiero ganar $ 2,000 más este mes en ingresos". De esa manera, sabes cuándo has completado la meta.

Todos los objetivos deben ser alcanzables. Una meta alcanzable es algo que usted puede lograr razonablemente. Si bien tener metas altas es genial, desea guardarlas a largo plazo. Mantenga sus objetivos actuales simples.

¿Es relevante tu objetivo? Piense en su enfoque de negocio y lo que desea lograr. Todos sus objetivos deben girar en torno a su negocio y la mejora de sus habilidades profesionales.

Finalmente, siempre agregue un período de tiempo a sus objetivos. De esa manera, puede esforzarse por completarlos mientras son relevantes para usted. Además, esto aumenta la productividad y evita que te saltes objetivos importantes.

Mantenerse productivo en casa

Como emprendedor en solitario, es probable que trabajes desde casa. Hay una gran diferencia entre un entorno de oficina y un home office. Puede ser normal tomar algún tiempo para adaptarse. Armamos algunos consejos para que te mantengas productivo en casa:

- Espacios de trabajo y de hogar separados
- Apegarse a una rutina
- Mantenga su área de trabajo ordenada
- Silencia tu teléfono
- Eliminar distracciones
- Empuje a través de los días lentos

- Mantener un planificador o calendario
- Tómese breves descansos
- Mantenga notas

Todos somos culpables de volver al trabajo cuando tenemos una buena idea. ¿Se te ocurrió una gran entrada de blog fuera de tus horas de trabajo? Tome nota de ello, luego vuelva a él al día siguiente. **Los solopreneurs necesitan tener un fuerte equilibrio entre el trabajo y la vida personal para mantenerse productivos.** Si sigues volviendo al trabajo, perderás tu rutina y también perderás tu motivación.

En su lugar, siempre lleve consigo un cuaderno y un bolígrafo. Siempre que tengas una idea, anótala. No tiene que organizarse; solo un pequeño libro en el que puede registrar sus ideas o planes de negocio cuando la inspiración llega. Si no desea llevar nada más con usted, siempre puede usar una aplicación de bloc de notas en su teléfono.

Aprenda sus horas de productividad

Finalmente, cada uno tiene diferentes horas de productividad. Algunos de nosotros somos más productivos por la mañana. Otros son noctámbulos o prefieren hacer la mayor parte de su trabajo en medio del día, cada uno es diferente.

Al trabajar cuando eres el más productivo, conseguirás hacer mucho más. Además, no se sentirá como si te estuvieras forzando a ti mismo. Sin embargo, primero debe aprender cuándo son sus horas de productividad. Le recomendamos que lleve un registro de cuándo se siente motivado durante unas semanas.

Si sus datos muestran que usted es productivo fuera de sus horas de trabajo, cambie su horario. Es probable que disfrutes mucho más trabajando durante ese otro tiempo. Este es uno de los beneficios más significativos que viene con ser su propio jefe. Si el 9 al 5 no funciona para ti, ¡cámbialo! Como solopreneur, usted puede ser productivo en su propio tiempo.

Pruebe primero una tarea pequeña

Si está posponiendo un proyecto grande en el que necesita trabajar, intente iniciar primero una tarea pequeña. Una vez que lo haya completado, va a ser mucho más fácil para usted pasar a la siguiente tarea. Ser productivo puede ser difícil de comenzar, pero una vez que te pones en marcha, es aún más difícil detenerlo.

Algunas tareas pequeñas incluyen responder a correos electrónicos, revisar las redes sociales de su marca o escribir publicaciones cortas. Inmediatamente después de terminar la tarea corta, pasar al gran proyecto. Usted debe notar una diferencia en su voluntad de empezar.

Estas pequeñas tareas deben tardar diez minutos como máximo en completarse. Si los estás haciendo por motivación, no quieres que distraigan del gran proyecto que necesita ser completado.

Network for Success

Capítulo 5: Red para el éxito

El networking es una de las tareas más importantes que realizarás como emprendedor en solitario. Al establecer contactos, mejorará su tráfico, conversiones y conciencia de la audiencia. Estos son los beneficios de construir una red sólida:

- Más referencias
- Nuevos Clientes
- Conoce a más solopreneurs
- Establecer una presencia profesional
- Construye tus habilidades y experiencia

Construyendo su red

Una de las maneras más fáciles de comenzar a construir su red es asistir a conferencias y seminarios. Cualquier entorno de taller donde sepas que habrá otros solopreneurs es el lugar perfecto para comenzar. Estos eventos son perfectos para hablar con otras personas en su campo.

Al asistir, te conectas con otros y construyes relaciones profesionales, lo que puede conducir fácilmente a redes sólidas. Quieres construir una comunidad que pueda ayudar a tu negocio a crecer y la mejor manera de hacerlo es simplemente ponerte ahí fuera.

A continuación, una vez que haya iniciado una pequeña red, querrá ramificarse. Puede pedirle a otros solopreneurs que le presenten o le proporcionen información de contacto.

Otra forma de construir una red fuerte es unirse a una organización. Hay un montón de grupos que se pueden encontrar en línea, así como en su área local.

Conéctese a través de las redes sociales

Como emprendedor en solitario, ya debe tener una cuenta de redes sociales creada para su negocio. Puede utilizar fácilmente esta cuenta para conectarse con otros y fortalecer su red. Plataformas como Facebook, Instagram y Twitter son perfectas para esto.

Para empezar, asegúrate de que tu perfil esté actualizado y de que tu empresa haya estado publicando contenido con frecuencia. Estos son algunos consejos de redes sociales para su perfil:

- Compruebe que todos los vínculos funcionan
- Usa hashtags relevantes
- Responder a los comentarios de manera oportuna
- Asegúrate de que tu información de contacto sea fácil de ver
- Todas las imágenes deben seguir la identidad de su marca y los temas de color

La página de redes sociales de un solopreneur siempre necesita ser actualizada. Usted querrá comprobar en él a menudo durante sus horas de trabajo, para asegurarse de que no se está perdiendo ninguna oportunidad de red. Si alguien se acerca a usted, usted querrá responder tan pronto como esté en línea.

Las redes sociales son una herramienta de redes increíble. Usted querrá utilizarlo a su máximo potencial. Si no tiene tiempo para dedicarse a la gestión de redes sociales, siempre puede externalizar esta tarea. Los administradores de redes sociales o un asistente virtual podrán ayudarlo en gran medida en este frente.

Construyendo tu audiencia

Otra parte esencial de la creación de redes incluye la construcción de su audiencia. Para hacer esto en línea, deberá hacer lo siguiente con las redes sociales de su marca:

- Agregar contenido de calidad regularmente
- Involucre a su audiencia con contenido
- Interactuar con ellos, es decir, comentar y me gusta mensajes
- Publicar contenido que sea relevante
- Prueba la publicidad en redes sociales
- Prueba a hacer videos o un podcast
- Desarrolla tus estrategias de marketing de contenidos

Al publicar e interactuar regularmente con su audiencia, notará que más personas interactúan con su marca. A medida que su audiencia crece, también lo hace su exposición, lo que es excelente para las redes de negocios.

Desea crear y cargar contenido que las personas querrán compartir, lo que significa que tendrá que dedicarle una buena cantidad de tiempo. Hay estudios de creación de contenido por ahí que harán videos para usted. También hay un montón de freelancers de escritura y diseño gráfico que podrían ayudarlo a crear una variedad de contenido.

Si tienes tiempo, también puedes hacer el contenido tú mismo. Usted querrá asegurarse de que todo lo que publique bajo el nombre de su marca es de alta calidad y convincente. Muchos solopreneurs que están comenzando harán una mayoría del contenido ellos mismos, hasta que puedan permitirse el lujo de externalizar más de su trabajo.

Realizar investigaciones

A continuación, querrá realizar una investigación sobre su audiencia. Tendrá que determinar quién es su objetivo demográfico y luego ir a partir de ahí. ¿Quiénes son sus clientes ideales? Querrá usar análisis para ver quién responde más al contenido de sus redes sociales.

Las herramientas de análisis se pueden usar para ver qué tipo de personas están viendo sus páginas. Puede utilizar esta información para crear ideas y contenido que se adapte a ellos. Al llevar a cabo su investigación, usted va a beneficiar a sus niveles de tráfico.

Además, la realización de investigaciones sobre su audiencia le ayudará en gran medida con la creación de redes. Usted tendrá la información de fondo necesaria para conocer a nuevos profesionales y expandir su negocio en línea.

La investigación para su negocio es algo en lo que desea poner mucho esfuerzo. Es posible que desee considerar hablar con consultores de negocios o un experto en SEO, ya que estos profesionales sabrán cómo ayudarlo a realizar investigaciones sobre su audiencia.

Hacer que las redes sean divertidas

Muchos solopreneurs odian las redes, ¡pero puede ser divertido! Si te sientes emocionado por conocer a la gente, ellos tendrán una mejor impresión de ti. Es posible que desee hablar sobre los planes de negocios durante la cena o organizar sus propios eventos. No importa lo que decidas hacer, siempre puedes pasar un buen rato con las redes.

Si eres un apasionado de tu negocio, se verá. Puede considerar organizar eventos que giren en torno a su enfoque empresarial y animen a otros a hacer preguntas sobre lo que hace. Al final del día, asegúrese de que la red de una manera que sea cómoda para usted.

Los eventos de networking no tienen por qué sentirse como "trabajo". Simplemente necesita reunirse con la gente y discutir su negocio, lo que significa que tiene espacio para convertirlo en un evento divertido.

Know When to Pay For Tools And When Not

Capítulo 6: Saber cuándo pagar por las herramientas ... Y cuándo no

Los solopreneurs a menudo tienen presupuestos estrictos, especialmente los que están empezando. Eso significa que querrá usar todos los recursos que tiene de manera efectiva. Ayuda saber cuándo debe pagar por usar herramientas y cuándo no.

Hay muchas herramientas diferentes por ahí. La mayoría de ellos ejecutan un sistema "freemium". Esto significa que son libres de usar algunas de sus características, pero tendrá que pagar para desbloquear todas las características a través de una cuenta premium.

Esto es lo que querrá considerar antes de comprar una herramienta.

¿Es útil?

¿Qué tan útil será la herramienta? No desea pagar por solo algunas características que usará, especialmente porque es probable que haya otras herramientas que cubrirán todo lo que necesita.

Es posible que desee hacer una lista de todas las cosas con las que la herramienta puede ayudarlo. Haga esto para varias opciones diferentes, luego compare los precios. Este proceso puede ayudarlo a determinar qué herramientas le están dando las características que necesitan, además de la etiqueta de precio que viene con él.

¿Con qué frecuencia lo usará?

Es posible que desee comprar algo que pueda usar todos los días. Si la herramienta sólo va a ser útil para usted una vez al mes, entonces no tendría sentido comprarlo. Las características deben ser las que ya sabe que va a recurrir a menudo.

¿Hay una versión gratuita?

Antes de comprar cualquier herramienta, siempre compruebe si hay una versión gratuita. En algunos casos, las características que necesita están detrás de un muro de pago con una herramienta, pero gratis en otra. Siempre asegúrese de hacer una investigación exhaustiva antes de ordenar nada. Es posible que pueda acceder a una herramienta muy similar de forma gratuita en algún otro lugar.

¿Se ajustará a su presupuesto?

Los solopreneurs tienen generalmente presupuestos terminantes que necesitan permanecer adentro para su negocio. Asegúrese de hacer referencia a su presupuesto antes de comprar cualquier herramienta, es posible que no tenga espacio para ello. Ayuda a comparar precios y buscar herramientas en línea gratuitas en otros lugares si algo parece ser un poco demasiado caro.

¿Se puede subcontratar?

Una persona profesional será capaz de ofrecerle mejores resultados finales que una herramienta en línea. Por ejemplo, si usa un contador independiente para crear su presupuesto, pueden considerar más factores que una aplicación de presupuesto. A medida que hable y trabaje con ellos, el profesional podrá ajustar y personalizar completamente su presupuesto para que se adapte a su negocio. Un programa no puede hacer esto.

Si está buscando construir su negocio aún más, debe subcontratar cuando sea posible. Si lo hace, ayudará a su red y le permitirá crecer aún más. Además, los profesionales pueden ofrecerte consejos reales que una herramienta no puede.

Por supuesto, tendrá que incluir la subcontratación en su presupuesto para que esto funcione. Si ya tiene herramientas que no está utilizando, es posible que desee cancelar las suscripciones. Cancelar puede dejarle con algunos fondos mensuales adicionales que podrían destinarse a la subcontratación de su trabajo en su lugar.

Ejemplos de herramientas en línea

Las herramientas en línea le proporcionan servicios que puede utilizar para promover sus negocios. Un ejemplo incluye Grammarly. Esta herramienta es un corrector en línea que comprueba su gramática, que es perfecto para la comunicación en línea.

Sin embargo, ¿pagarías por una suscripción? Esta herramienta es útil. La versión gratuita ya podría cubrir todo lo que necesita. Si desea una revisión gramatical simple, entonces valdría la pena usarlo. Muchos escritores de solopreneur utilizan la versión de pago de esta herramienta. Es útil para ellos porque proporciona correcciones gramaticales, un verificador de plagio y sugerencias para agregar más estilo a su trabajo.

Una de las herramientas más populares es Slack. Le permite mantenerse fácilmente en contacto con otros profesionales. Podría considerar usarlo para organizarlo y comunicarse con los profesionales a los que está subcontratando el trabajo. La aplicación tiene un montón de usos para organizar sus reuniones de red, así.

Otras herramientas pueden rastrear su millaje para el trabajo, rastrear sus finanzas y ofrecer información de SEO. Hay un montón de herramientas por ahí. Si necesita ayuda, probablemente pueda encontrar algo en línea para ayudarlo.

En general, querrá investigar herramientas y comparar sus costos con su presupuesto. Desea ahorrar dinero donde pueda, pero use herramientas que le sean útiles. Si crees que una herramienta expandirá tu red, te dará una mayor audiencia de clientes o te permitirá llegar a más clientes, vale la pena obtenerla.

Capítulo 7: Concéntrese en el progreso, no en la perfección

Los solopreneurs a menudo pueden obsesionarse con la perfección. Es fácil de hacer: quieres que tu negocio sea lo mejor que pueda ser. Sin embargo, es importante darse cuenta de que el progreso es más importante que la perfección. De hecho, el perfeccionismo podría estar obstaculizando su negocio.

Los solopreneurs exitosos llevaron su trabajo un paso a la vez para llegar a donde están hoy. Tendrás que hacer lo mismo. Se necesitan años para construir el negocio perfecto, no se puede esperar que aparezca de la noche a la mañana!

Por qué no quieres perfeccionismo

Ser un perfeccionista puede ralentizar en gran medida su flujo de trabajo. Puede hacer que pierda su tiempo y reduzca su productividad. Si sabes que vas a necesitar pasar mucho tiempo haciendo algo perfecto, puede ser mucho más difícil trabajar en ello.

Los perfeccionistas siempre están descontentos con su trabajo. Esto les causa mucho estrés y preocupación. Pronto, comenzará a sentir que nada de lo que haces es lo suficientemente bueno, lo cual es una mentalidad horrible. Si te sientes de esta manera, nunca te sentirás satisfecho con tu trabajo.

Para mantenerte feliz y saludable, querrás una mentalidad más positiva. En lugar de enfocarse en la perfección, ponga su enfoque en progresar. Trate de hacerlo mejor cada día. Quieres mejorar cada vez que haces algo para un cliente o un cliente.

Además, es mucho más fácil medir su progreso que saber si algo es perfecto. Por supuesto, eso no significa que no debas poner todo tu esfuerzo en el trabajo que haces.

Además, si sientes que tu trabajo es de calidad, tu audiencia se dará cuenta de inmediato. Es mejor tener confianza en todo lo que haces y haces por tu negocio.

La perfección es imposible

La perfección es imposible de alcanzar. Incluso los solopreneurs más conocidos no son perfectos. El perfeccionismo incluye estándares increíblemente altos que nunca se pueden alcanzar. Cuando alcanzas una determinada meta con tu trabajo, luego continúa rehaciéndolo para tratar de "perfeccionarlo", es probable que sientas que no estás alcanzando el estándar que estableciste para ti mismo.

El perfeccionismo tiene un impacto negativo en la salud mental de las personas. Puede hacer que te sientas insatisfecho e inseguro de la calidad de tu trabajo. Con el tiempo, esto podría incluso hacerte sentir sin valor.

En su lugar, querrá centrarse en los aspectos positivos. **Considere cada nuevo trabajo o venta una experiencia de aprendizaje.** Una vez que hayas completado el proyecto, sabrás que el próximo que hagas será aún mejor.

Cómo centrarse en el progreso

Puede ser difícil para usted ver su progreso al principio. Comience por mirar el panorama general. ¿Estás logrando más metas? ¿Está creciendo tu audiencia?

¿Estás conociendo y trabajando con nuevos clientes? Si lo estás, entonces estás progresando con tu negocio.

Querrás hacerte responsable del trabajo que haces, esto no significa ser un perfeccionista. En su lugar, querrá hacer el mejor trabajo que pueda, en el marco de tiempo que tenga. Si bien es probable que se necesiten algunas revisiones, no desea volver a trabajar todo constantemente. Esto lo dejará sintiéndose agotado y podría comenzar a resentirse de su negocio.

A continuación, celebre todas sus victorias, grandes y pequeñas. Esto hará que todas sus metas se sientan importantes y le dará tiempo para sentirse bien con el trabajo duro que está haciendo. ¡Confía en nosotros, mereces celebrarlo!

Cómo realizar un seguimiento de su progreso

Entonces, ahora sabes por qué es importante hacer un seguimiento de tu progreso, pero ¿cómo lo haces realmente? Querrás reservar una pequeña porción de tiempo cada día que trabajes, para que puedas registrar tu progreso.

En lugar de solo cruzar un elemento de tu lista de tareas pendientes cuando esté completa, querrás dividirlo en objetivos más pequeños. Por ejemplo, en lugar de "Terminar proyecto de fotografía" le gustaría dividirlo en objetivos diarios. "Tomar fotos, editar fotos, finalizar y enviar al cliente" es mucho mejor.

Al dividir un gran proyecto en objetivos más pequeños, también te estás permitiendo celebrar pequeñas victorias. Además, puede ver qué pasos deben terminarse aún, lo que le permite administrar su tiempo de manera mucho más eficiente.

Puede realizar un seguimiento de su progreso en aplicaciones o en un bloc de notas. Asegúrese de registrar todos sus logros, ya sean grandes o pequeños. Al final de cada semana, puede revisar lo que logró. A partir de ahí, puede determinar cuáles deben ser sus objetivos para la próxima semana. Para seguir progresando, siempre querrás seguir construyendo tus metas.

Don't Forget Your Off Time

Capítulo 8: No olvides tu tiempo libre

Los solopreneurs necesitan tener un fuerte equilibrio entre el trabajo y la vida personal. Trabajar desde casa puede hacer que su carrera se sienta intrusiva en su vida doméstica. Necesitas separar los dos si quieres mantenerte motivado y evitar distracciones.

Además, si no está tomando descansos, rápidamente se verá abrumado por el trabajo. Cuando eso sucede, tu motivación puede desaparecer, dejándolo con mucho trabajo por hacer, pero sin impulso para completarlo.

Cómo tomar descansos

Puede parecer una tontería incluir esta sección, pero a muchos solopreneurs les encanta trabajar. Si bien esto es bueno, debe saber cómo tomar descansos para evitar el agotamiento. Comience por incluir descansos en su horario de trabajo. Durante sus descansos, asegúrese de apagar su teléfono y no revise los correos electrónicos de trabajo. Simplemente relájate y haz lo que quieras hasta que llegue el momento de volver al trabajo.

Asegúrese de dejar que otros sepan cuál es su horario. De esa manera, tus freelancers y clientes no se confunden cuando no respondes de inmediato. Muchas herramientas le permiten establecer su estado en "Ausente", lo que es muy útil para la comunicación. Hacerlo también le permite establecer límites saludables entre el trabajo y la vida.

Siempre utilice su descanso como un descanso. No quieres seguir trabajando durante ella, ya que esto podría hacerte sentirte rápidamente quemado. Tomar descansos puede ayudarte a ser más productivo y debería hacerte sentir renovado.

Qué hacer en su descanso

A veces, puede ser demasiado tentador hacer otras cosas estresantes en nuestros descansos. Es posible que desee hacer platos o la ropa, pero pueden tomar demasiado tiempo. Esto te dejaría sin un momento para ti mismo para recoger tus pensamientos y recargar energías.

Estas son algunas ideas para sus descansos de trabajo:

- Comienza un pasatiempo de descanso
    - Tejer
    - Proyectos artísticos
    - Edificio
- Coma un refrigerio saludable
- meditación
- Dar un paseo
- elasticidad
- Hable con un ser querido
- Juega con tu mascota
- Siesta de alimentación

Cualquier actividad que puedas hacer en 10 minutos que te deje feliz, refrescado y relajado puede ser considerada. Todo el mundo disfruta haciendo cosas diferentes, por lo que sabrá qué hacer mejor!

Por ejemplo, tejer es un pasatiempo relajante. Si trabajaste en tu pieza durante 10 minutos seguidos en tus descansos, podrías hacer gran parte del proyecto en un día. El movimiento repetitivo también es extremadamente calmante para muchas personas. Si siente que necesita tomar una siesta, asegúrese de tomar una siesta de energía. Si vas

durante 20 minutos, puede sentirse aturdido e incluso más cansado que antes.

Mientras no lleves tu trabajo a tus descansos, estarás bien. Esto incluye responder a correos electrónicos y mensajes de trabajo, así que asegúrese de silenciar su teléfono celular hasta que termine su descanso.

Por qué necesitamos descansos de trabajo

Incluso trabajar desde casa es estresante. Los solopreneurs necesitan saber cuándo dar un paso atrás en su negocio. Si no lo hace, entonces es probable que se sienta agitado y fatigado al final del día. Solo puedes ser así durante tanto tiempo antes de que algo se rompa o comiences a odiar tu carrera.

Las pausas de trabajo reducen nuestro estrés. Esto le permite alejarse de sus desafíos diarios y disfrutar de un refrigerio o visita con su familia. Una vez que vuelvas al trabajo, podrás manejar el siguiente proyecto con la mente clara. A menudo, puede llegar a más ideas después de alejarse de una tarea difícil.

Eso le permitirá ser aún más productivo. En general, nunca debe omitir los descansos, incluso mientras trabaja de forma remota. El estrés crónico puede causar un impacto negativo en su salud física y mental, por lo que querrá evitarlo cuando sea posible.

¿Cuánto tiempo debe ser su descanso?

Si toma un descanso que es demasiado largo, puede ser difícil volver al trabajo. En su lugar, desea encontrar un término medio que lo deje renovado, sin pasarse por la borda. La investigación apunta a que los descansos más cortos son mejores para la productividad.

Ayuda si toma descansos de acuerdo con el tiempo que trabajó. Por ejemplo, si ha trabajado durante minutos, tómese un descanso de cinco minutos. Si trabajó durante dos horas, es posible que desee tomar un descanso de 30 minutos. Dependerá del tipo de proyectos que esté realizando también.

Los solopreneurs tienen la ventaja de poder elegir cuando toman sus descansos. Este beneficio te permitirá trabajar durante los momentos en que seas más productivo y tomar descansos a medida que los necesites. Una vez más, asegúrese de que su "tiempo de descanso" no se convierte accidentalmente en "tiempo de trabajo"!

Aumentar la productividad

Los descansos son esenciales para aumentar su motivación y, por lo tanto, su productividad. Te dan la oportunidad de relajarte, luego te permiten trabajar en la tarea con una mente clara. Muchos solopreneurs exitosos se toman sus descansos muy en serio, ¡así que deberías hacerlo!

Si desea aumentar su productividad, asegúrese de tomar descansos a menudo durante todo el día. Es probable que deba experimentar para determinar qué tiempos van a funcionar mejor para usted.

Conclusion

conclusión

Ser un solopreneur es una de las trayectorias profesionales más satisfactorias que existen. Puedes enfocarte en construir un negocio a partir de algo que te apasiona. Muchos solopreneurs aman su trabajo y disfrutan de lo que hacen.

Además, muchos están contentos de no tener que reportar a un jefe más. Si te sientes listo para salir de los campos tradicionales de trabajo y quieres establecer tus propios horarios, entonces convertirte en un solopreneur podría ser la mejor profesión para ti.

Los solopreneurs necesitan saber cómo tener autodisciplina. Si está constantemente distraído y procrastinando, entonces nada con su negocio se terminará nunca. Usted necesita tener un fuerte equilibrio entre el trabajo y la vida con el fin de lograr todas sus tareas y objetivos diarios.

Sin embargo, si usted puede hacer eso, entonces usted puede ejecutar un negocio exitoso! Esperamos que hayas aprendido mucho de este libro. Asegúrese de comunicarse con nosotros si tiene alguna pregunta. También hay mucha más información para solopreneurs en nuestro sitio web que usted puede estar interesado en!

Sobre el autor

C.X. Cruz nació en Puerto Rico y ha vivido en el área de la ciudad de Nueva York desde que tenía 14 años. Tiene títulos de posgrado de la Universidad Estatal de Nueva York y la Universidad de Honolulu en Ciencias de la Computación. Ha trabajado para bancos de inversión europeos como UBS, y para bancos estadounidenses como Goldman Sachs. Sus aficiones incluyen la silvicultura y el remo.

Cuando era un estudiante de posgrado muy joven, Cruz pensó en publicar libros. Hace 30 años era extremadamente difícil publicar un libro utilizando los métodos tradicionales. Renunció a este sueño editorial en ese entonces. Afortunadamente, hay numerosas maneras de convertirse en un auto-editor hoy en día. Internet ha democratizado muchos negocios como la edición de libros. Cruz puede traerte un gran contenido y un gran precio. Nunca dejes de leer y aprender. ¡Cruz sabe que disfrutarás leyendo sus libros!

legal

El material de este libro se obtuvo de InDigitalWorks.com con el Derecho de Participación Principal.

Sin responsabilidad

Bajo ninguna circunstancia el creador del producto, programador o cualquiera de los distribuidores de este producto, o cualquier distribuidor, será responsable ante cualquier parte por cualquier daño directo, indirecto, punitivo, especial, incidental u otro daño consecuente que surja directa o indirectamente del uso de este producto. Este producto se proporciona "tal cual" y sin garantías.

El uso de este producto indica su aceptación de la política de "No responsabilidad". Si no está de acuerdo con nuestra política de "No responsabilidad", entonces no se le permite usar o distribuir este producto (si corresponde). La falta de lectura de este aviso en su totalidad no anula su aceptación de esta política en caso de que decida utilizar este producto.

La ley aplicable puede no permitir la limitación o exclusión de responsabilidad o daños incidentales o consecuentes, por lo que la limitación o exclusión anterior puede no aplicarse a usted. La responsabilidad por daños y perjuicios, independientemente de la forma de la acción, no excederá la tarifa real pagada por el producto.

InDigitalWorks.com

derechos de autor

Copyright © 2021 CX Cruz Autoedición Todos los derechos reservados.

Ninguna parte de esta publicación puede ser reproducida, distribuida o transmitida en cualquier forma o por cualquier medio, incluyendo fotocopias, grabaciones u otros métodos electrónicos o mecánicos, sin el permiso previo por escrito del editor, excepto en el caso de citas breves incorporadas en revisiones y ciertos otros usos no comerciales permitidos por la ley de derechos de autor. La responsabilidad por daños y perjuicios, independientemente de la forma de la acción, no excederá la tarifa real pagada por el producto. Este libro electrónico ha sido escrito únicamente con fines informativos.

AI Resume Analysis: Using AI to identify strengths and weaknesses in your current resume...........37
Lesson 3: Rewriting and Refining with AI 40
   AI-Assisted Rewriting: Implementing AI suggestions to improve phrasing and impact.................... 40
   Formatting for Success: Understanding how AI can suggest effective resume layouts. 41
Lesson 4: Tailoring Your Resume for the Job 43
   Job Description Analysis: Leveraging AI to tailor your resume to specific job postings..................... 43
   Competitive Edge: How AI compares your resume to others in the field. 43
Lesson 5: Finalizing Your AI-Enhanced Resume... 44
   Error Checking: Utilizing AI for grammar and consistency checks. 44
   AI Review and Feedback: Getting a final critique from an AI tool.. 45

Module 1: Personal Branding in the Digital Age

Lesson 1: The Power of Personal Branding

Introduction to Personal Branding: Defining personal branding and its importance in the digital era.

Understanding Personal Branding Personal branding is the intentional and strategic practice of marketing yourself. It's about creating a unique image and reputation that reflects your values, skills, and passions. In the digital age, where everyone has access to a global audience through social media and other online platforms, personal branding has become more crucial than ever.

Why Personal Branding Matters

- **Differentiation**: It sets you apart from the competition, highlighting what makes you unique.
- **Opportunity**: A strong personal brand can attract career opportunities that align with your strengths and interests.
- **Control:** You control the narrative around your professional image, ensuring it's accurate, coherent, and compelling.

Creating Your Personal Brand

1. **Identify Your Unique Value Proposition**: What are your core values? What do you excel at? What do you want to be known for?
2. **Develop Your Online Presence**: Choose platforms that play to your strengths and commit to them. Whether it's a blog, podcast, or social media, consistency is key.
3. **Content Creation**: Share your knowledge and experiences through various forms of content. <u>Long-form content can be repurposed into bite-sized pieces for broader reach.</u>

AI Tools for Career Development AI tools can significantly enhance your career development efforts by providing personalized insights, automating tasks, and optimizing your professional presence online. Here are some ways AI can assist you:

- **Resume Building**: AI can help tailor your resume to highlight relevant skills and optimize for industry keywords.
- **Interview Preparation**: AI-powered mock interviews and interview coaching can prepare you for real-world scenarios.
- **Professional Networking**: AI can assist in crafting personalized messages for LinkedIn or other networking platforms.

- **Key Elements of a Personal Brand**: Identifying the components that make up a strong personal brand.
- **Activity**: Participants will list their core values, strengths, and professional aspirations to begin shaping their personal brand narrative.

Lesson 2: Crafting Your Digital Persona

Creating a Cohesive Online Presence: Strategies for aligning your online profiles with your personal brand.

1. Understanding Your Digital Persona Your digital persona is the online representation of your personal brand. It's how you present yourself on various digital platforms and how others perceive you. It's crafted through:

- **Your Content**: What you post, share, and comment on.
- **Your Interactions**: How you engage with others online.
- **Your Visuals**: The images, videos, and overall aesthetics of your profiles.

2. Aligning Your Persona with Your Goals To craft an effective digital persona, align it with your professional and personal goals. Ask yourself:

- What are my career objectives?
- How do I want to be perceived by my peers and potential employers or clients?
- Which aspects of my personality and expertise do I want to highlight?

3. Content is King Content creation is at the heart of crafting your digital persona. Your content should:

- **Reflect Your Expertise**: Share insights and knowledge that showcase your skills.
- **Be Consistent with Your Brand**: Ensure your content aligns with your brand's voice and values.
- **Engage Your Audience**: Create content that resonates with your followers and encourages interaction.

4. Developing a Content Strategy A content strategy helps you plan and execute your online presence. It involves:

- **Content Calendar**: Schedule your posts to maintain a consistent presence.
- **Content Mix**: Balance original content with curated content that adds value to your audience.
- **Analytics**: Use tools to analyze the performance of your content and adjust your strategy accordingly.

5. Engagement and Authenticity Engagement is crucial for building a community around your brand. To engage authentically:

- **Be Responsive**: Reply to comments and messages promptly.
- **Be Genuine**: Share your true thoughts and opinions.
- **Be Transparent**: Let your audience see the person behind the brand.

6. Leveraging AI Tools AI tools can help you craft and maintain your digital persona by:

- **Analyzing Your Online Presence**: Providing insights into how you're perceived online.
- **Optimizing Your Content**: Suggesting the best times to post and the types of content that perform well.
- **Personalizing Your Interactions**: Helping you maintain a personalized touch at scale.

7. **Monitoring and Adapting** Your digital persona is not static. It's important to:

- **Monitor Your Online Presence**: Keep an eye on how your content is received and what's being said about you.
- **Adapt to Feedback**: Be willing to make changes based on the responses you get.
- **Stay Current**: Keep up with trends and adjust your persona as needed.

- **Optimizing Social Media Profiles**: Tips for enhancing LinkedIn, Twitter, and other social media platforms.

Activity: A step-by-step guide to revamping a LinkedIn profile, with a focus on headline, summary, and experience sections.

Objective: Utilize AI tools to optimize your LinkedIn profile, making it more attractive to recruiters and potential connections.

Materials Needed:

- Access to AI-powered writing assistants.
- Access to LinkedIn profile analytics tools.
- A list of industry-specific keywords.

Step 1: Optimizing Your Headline

- **Task**: Use an AI writing assistant to generate several headline options.
- **Action**: Input your job title, skills, and desired industry into the AI tool to produce compelling headlines.
- **Outcome**: Select the headline that best represents your professional identity and goals.
- **Prompt**: "Generate a professional headline for a [Your Job Title] who specializes in [Your Skills] and is looking to advance in the [Your Industry]."

Step 2: Crafting a Powerful Summary

- **Task**: Analyze successful LinkedIn summaries in your field with AI analytics tools.
- **Action**: Identify common patterns and keywords that resonate with your industry.
- **Outcome**: Draft a summary that tells your professional story and incorporates these elements.
- **Prompt**: "Write a brief professional summary for a [Your Job Title] with experience in [Your Skills/Industry]. Include a hook, a narrative of career progression, and a call to action."

Step 3: Enhancing Your Experience Section

- **Task**: Leverage AI to quantify your achievements.
- **Action**: Input your career achievements into the AI tool to receive suggestions on how to quantify and present them effectively.
- **Outcome**: Update your experience section with data-driven results that showcase your impact.

Step 4: Refining with AI Feedback

- **Task**: Use AI-powered LinkedIn profile optimization tools to get feedback on your profile.
- **Action**: Implement the suggested changes to improve your profile's visibility and appeal.
- **Outcome**: A fully optimized LinkedIn profile that stands out in your industry.

Reflection:

- Reflect on how AI tools have streamlined the process of profile optimization.
- Consider the changes in profile views and connection requests since the revamp.

By completing this activity, you'll not only have a LinkedIn profile that's tailored for career growth but also gain insights into how AI tools can be leveraged for professional development. Remember, the key is to maintain an authentic and updated profile that truly reflects your professional journey and aspirations. Good luck!

Lesson 3: AI-Assisted Content Creation

Leveraging AI for Content Development: Exploring AI tools that assist in creating blog posts, articles, and social media content.

Understanding AI in Content Creation

AI and Content Creation: AI tools are revolutionizing content creation by providing assistance in generating ideas, structuring articles, and even crafting entire pieces of content. These tools use advanced algorithms to analyze data, understand context, and produce relevant content suggestions.

Selecting the Right AI Tools

Identifying Your Needs: Before diving into AI tools, it's crucial to identify your content needs. Are you looking to generate ideas, improve grammar, or automate social media posts? Your needs will dictate which AI tools will be most beneficial for you.

AI Tool Categories:

- **Idea Generation**: Tools that help brainstorm topics, headlines, and angles.
- **Content Drafting**: Platforms that assist in writing drafts with suggestions for tone, style, and structure.
- **Editing and Refinement**: Software that offers grammar checks, style edits, and plagiarism detection.

- **Social Media Management**: Applications that schedule posts, analyze performance, and suggest content improvements.

Integrating AI into Your Writing Process

Step-by-Step Integration:

1. **Start with Research**: Use AI to gather data on trending topics and keywords within your industry.
2. **Create a Draft**: Leverage AI to help outline your article or blog post and provide suggestions for content flow.
3. **Edit and Refine**: Employ AI tools for grammar checks and style suggestions to polish your content.
4. **Schedule and Analyze**: For social media, use AI to determine the best times to post and to analyze the engagement data.

Enhancing Digital Presence with AI

Consistency is Key: Regularly updated content is vital for digital presence. AI can help maintain a consistent posting schedule across various platforms.

Engagement and SEO: AI tools can optimize your content for search engines and suggest ways to increase user engagement.

Personal Touch: While AI provides a solid foundation, adding your personal insights and experiences will make your content stand out.

Practical Tips for Using AI Tools

- **Activity**: Using an AI tool to generate a blog post outline on a topic related to the participant's industry.

Objective: To familiarize participants with AI tools for creating structured outlines for blog posts that are pertinent to their professional field.

Step-by-Step Guide:

1. **Topic Selection**:
   - **Task**: Choose a topic that is both relevant to your industry and of interest to your target audience.
   - **Tips**: Consider current trends, common challenges, or emerging technologies within your field.
2. **AI Tool Familiarization**:
   - **Task**: Get to know the AI tool you will be using. Understand its features and how it can assist in content creation.
   - **Tips**: Look for tools that offer flexibility in content generation and support for various content types.
3. **Generating the Outline**:
   - **Task**: Use the AI tool to input your topic and generate a list of key points, questions, or themes to cover.
   - **Tips**: Use the AI-generated points as a starting place, and don't be afraid to modify them to better suit your needs.
4. **Outline Structuring**:

- Task: Organize the AI-generated ideas into a coherent outline. This should include an introduction, main points with subheadings, and a conclusion.
    - Tips: Ensure that the outline flows logically and covers the topic comprehensively
5. **Personalization**:
    - Task: Add your personal insights, experiences, or case studies to the outline to provide depth and authenticity.
    - Tips: Think about how your personal touch can add value to the content and resonate with your audience.
6. **Review and Refinement**:
    - Task: Review the outline for coherence, relevance, and interest. Refine it to ensure it meets the standards of your brand and industry.
    - Tips: Consider getting feedback from peers or mentors to further improve the outline.

Lesson 4: Maintaining Your Brand Over Time

- **Consistency and Authenticity**: Keeping your personal brand consistent across all platforms while remaining authentic.
- **Personal Brand Evolution**: How to evolve your brand as your career grows.
- **Activity**: Develop a personal brand refresh plan that participants can implement annually.

Resources

- A list of AI tools for personal branding, including content creation, social media management, and analytics.

Content Creation Tools:

- **Jasper**: An AI writing assistant that helps generate ideas and create content for various platforms
- **Grammarly**: Offers writing assistance to ensure your content is grammatically correct and clear
- **Canva**: Provides design templates and tools to create visual content that aligns with your brand
- **Lumen5**: A video creation platform that turns blog posts and content into engaging videos

Social Media Management Tools:

- **Hootsuite**: Assists in scheduling posts, monitoring trends, and gaining insights into audience preferences
- **Buffer**: Tailors posts to each social media channel and offers analytics on performance
- **Publer**: Generates post text and images, helping to maintain a consistent posting schedule
- **Taplio**: Focuses on growing a personal brand on LinkedIn with content suggestions and engagement strategies

Analytics Tools:

- **Polymer**: Offers no-code AI visualization for analyzing social media and content performance

- **Tableau**: *An interactive data platform that provides insights into audience behavior and content engagement*
- **Microsoft Power BI**: *A business intelligence solution that can track and analyze your brand's online presence*
- **MonkeyLearn**: *Utilizes AI-powered text analysis to understand audience sentiment and content impact*

<mark>Templates for LinkedIn profile optimization, content calendars, and engagement analysis reports.</mark>

Headline: *[Your Professional Tagline | Your Expertise | Your Value Proposition]*

About Section: *(Be always clear to your goals, current projects, Unique Selling Point) remember, you are selling yourself, your image, you as a brand*

[Your Name] - [Your Current Position] at [Your Company]

With [X] years of experience in [Your Industry], I specialize in [Your Specialization]. I'm passionate about [Your Passion], and I'm known for [Your Unique Selling Point]. Currently, I'm focused on [Your Current Project/Goal].

Let's connect if you're interested in [Topics for Connection], or if you need expertise in [Your Expertise Areas].

Experience Section:

[Job Title]

[Company Name] - [Location] | [Month Year] - Present

- Achievement 1: [Description]

- Achievement 2: [Description]

- Key Skill: [Description]

[Previous Job Title]

[Previous Company Name] - [Location] | [Month Year] - [Month Year]

- Achievement 1: [Description]

- *Achievement 2: [Description]*

- *Key Skill: [Description]*

Recommendation Section:

Ask for recommendations from:

- *Former managers*

- *Colleagues*

- *Clients*

Assignments

- **Assignment 1**: Complete a LinkedIn profile optimization based on the strategies discussed in Lesson 2.
- **Assignment 2**: Create a content strategy for the next quarter using an AI tool, complete with topics, formats, and posting schedule.
- **Assignment 3**: Write and publish a blog post using an AI-generated outline and track its performance over two weeks.

Assessment

- Peer review of LinkedIn profile optimizations and content strategies.

Module 2: Strategic Networking with AI

Lesson 1: The Fundamentals of Networking

Networking Basics: Understanding the importance of networking in professional growth.

Networking is the cornerstone of professional development. It's about building a web of relationships that can provide support, feedback, information, and potential pathways to new opportunities. Here's a detailed look at why networking is so crucial:

- **Expanding Opportunities**: Networking can open doors to job offers, client leads, partnerships, and more that you might not find through traditional channels.
- **Exchange of Ideas**: It allows for the exchange of ideas, which can lead to innovations and improvements in your work.

- **Professional Support**: A strong network provides a sounding board for advice and support from peers and mentors.
- **Visibility**: Being active in professional circles increases your visibility and can establish you as a thought leader in your field.
- **Access to Resources**: Networks can provide access to resources and knowledge that are not readily available elsewhere.
- **Career Guidance**: Networking can offer guidance and insight into career moves and decisions.
- **Learning and Development**: It provides continuous learning opportunities from more experienced professionals.
- **Personal Branding**: It helps in building and maintaining a personal brand within your industry.

In the age of AI, networking has taken on new dimensions. AI tools can help identify potential connections, suggest networking events, and even recommend conversation starters. They can analyze your professional interests and align you with like-minded individuals or groups. AI can also keep track of your networking activities and prompt you when it's time to reach out or follow up with contacts.

Strategic networking with AI means leveraging technology to enhance these fundamental aspects of networking, making the process more efficient and effective. It's about using AI not just to connect with more people, but to connect with the right people in smarter ways.

In the next lessons, we'll explore how to strategically apply AI tools to your networking efforts, ensuring that you're building meaningful connections that will support your professional growth.

- **AI and Networking**: How AI is transforming traditional networking practices.

The advent of AI has brought a paradigm shift in the way professionals' network. Here's an in-depth look at how AI is transforming traditional networking practices:
- **Intelligent Matchmaking**: AI algorithms can analyze your professional profile, interests, and goals to suggest the most relevant connections, much like a matchmaking service for your career.
- **Event Recommendations**: AI can scour through vast databases of events and recommend networking opportunities that align with your professional interests, saving you time and increasing the likelihood of fruitful connections.
- **Communication Optimization**: AI tools can help craft personalized messages and suggest the optimal time to reach out to new contacts, increasing the chances of a positive response.
- **Social Media Insights**: AI-driven analytics tools can evaluate your social media activity, providing insights into how to improve your engagement and expand your professional network online.
- **Follow-Up Automation**: AI can remind you to follow up with new contacts at appropriate intervals, helping to maintain and strengthen your professional relationships.
- **Virtual Networking Assistants**: AI-powered chatbots can serve as virtual networking assistants, initiating conversations and managing interactions on your behalf.
- **Predictive Analytics**: AI can predict which connections are likely to be most beneficial for your career advancement, allowing you to focus your networking efforts more strategically.
- **Enhanced Learning**: AI-curated learning paths can help you acquire new skills that are in demand within your network, making you a more valuable connection.
- **Real-Time Language Translation**: For global networking, AI can break down language barriers by providing real-time translation, making it easier to connect with professionals from around the world.

> *By integrating AI into networking strategies, professionals can navigate the networking landscape more efficiently and effectively. AI doesn't just streamline the process; it enhances the quality of connections and interactions, ensuring that every handshake, virtual or otherwise, has the potential to lead to meaningful professional growth.*

- **Activity**: Identify personal networking goals and potential AI tools to assist in achieving them.

-
- **Ceiling**: An innovative AI-powered networking tool that facilitates professional connections
- **InProfiler**: An AI-driven LinkedIn lead profiling tool that categorizes and assesses connection requests based on professional goals
- **PenPal**: An eco-friendly AI networking tool featuring a digital NFC business card for easy sharing of contact information
- **LinkPlus**: A tool that helps expand your professional network by identifying and suggesting relevant connections
- **Resume Worded**: Offers AI-powered feedback on resumes and LinkedIn profiles to improve your professional appeal
- **DotsPal**: Connects professionals through AI-driven networking events and meetups
- **NetworkAI**: Assists in crafting powerful networking messages and optimizing your LinkedIn profile
- **MyPortfolio**: An AI tool that helps create a professional portfolio to showcase your skills and experience

- **Smart Networking Strategies**: Using AI to analyze and select the most beneficial networking events and online forums.
- **Activity**: Use an AI networking platform to create a list of potential contacts in your industry.

Objective: Utilize an AI networking platform to identify and create a list of potential contacts within your industry.

Tools Needed: Access to an AI networking platform (such as LinkedIn with AI-powered features or a specialized AI networking tool).

Instructions:
1. **Platform Selection**:
   - Choose an AI networking platform that is known for its robust AI features and is relevant to your industry.
   - Ensure you have a complete and professional profile set up on the platform.
2. **Defining Your Goals**:
   - Clearly define what you are looking to achieve through networking. It could be finding a mentor, expanding your professional network, or seeking new business opportunities.

- Identify the types of professionals you want to connect with, such as peers, industry leaders, potential clients, or collaborators.

3. **AI-Powered Search:**
   - Use the platform's AI search functionality to find individuals who match your defined goals and criteria.
   - Utilize filters such as location, current company, experience, and mutual connections to refine your search.

4. **Engagement Strategy:**
   - Develop a personalized engagement strategy for each potential contact. This could include a personalized connection request, a comment on a recent post they've made, or an invitation to a virtual networking event.

5. **Creating the List:**
   - As you identify potential contacts, add them to a list. Include their name, current position, company, and a note on why you've identified them as a valuable contact.
   - Organize the list by priority or by the type of connection they represent (mentor, peer, potential client, etc.).

6. **Initial Outreach:**
   - Craft personalized messages for outreach using AI suggestions for effective communication.
   - Keep track of who you've contacted, the date of outreach, and any responses received.

7. **Follow-Up:**
   - Set reminders to follow up with contacts who have not responded within a reasonable time frame.
   - Use the platform's AI features to suggest the best times for follow-up based on the contact's online activity patterns.

Expected Outcome:

By the end of this activity, you will have a curated list of potential contacts in your industry, along with a strategic plan for engaging with them. This list will serve as a foundation for expanding your professional network and opening up new opportunities for career growth.

Reflection:

After completing the activity, reflect on the process:

- How effective was the AI in identifying potential contacts?
- What strategies worked best for engaging with new contacts?
- How will you integrate this approach into your ongoing networking efforts?

- **Maintaining Relationships:** Utilizing AI to keep track of interactions and follow-ups.
- **Activity:** Draft a personalized outreach message using an AI writing assistant.

Lesson 2: Networking Etiquette and Best Practices

- **Digital Etiquette:** Understanding the do's and don'ts of online networking.

Digital Etiquette *refers to the set of social norms and expectations that govern appropriate behavior when using digital technologies. It's crucial for maintaining a professional and respectful online presence. Here are some key points to consider:*

- **Be Respectful and Courteous**: Always use appropriate language and tone when communicating online.
- **Mind Your Content**: Share content thoughtfully, considering its impact and appropriateness.
- **Avoid Sarcasm**: It can often be misinterpreted online due to the absence of vocal tone.
- **Respect Privacy**: Do not share personal information without consent.
- **Professionalism**: Maintain a professional image in all online interactions.
- **Think Before You Post**: Remember that everything online is permanent and can affect your reputation!

Best Practices: **Learning from AI-Generated Case Studies of Successful Networking Campaigns**

AI-generated case studies provide valuable insights into successful networking campaigns. Here are some best practices derived from these studies:

- **Heinz A.I. Ketchup Campaign**: Utilized AI to generate creative visuals, resulting in high global engagement and brand participation.
- **Nike's AI-Driven Campaign**: Showcased the importance of integrating AI to stay culturally relevant and appeal to a global audience.
- **Leverage AI for Personalization**: AI tools can help tailor your networking messages and strategies to specific audience segments, enhancing engagement.
- **Innovative AI Approaches**: Embrace AI-driven innovations to stand out and resonate across international markets.

By understanding digital etiquette and learning from AI-generated case studies, professionals can enhance their networking strategies and maintain a strong digital presence. These best practices serve as a guide to navigate the complexities of online networking while leveraging AI to maximize success.

Resources

- *Templates for outreach messages and follow-up emails.*

Outreach Message Templates

Version 1: Casual Introduction

Subject: *Let's Connect!*

Hi [Name],

I came across your profile and noticed our shared interest in [Specific Area]. As someone passionate about [Shared Interest], I'd love to connect and learn more about your experiences. Looking forward to connecting!

Best regards, [Your Name] [LinkedIn Profile]

Version 2: Mutual Goals

Subject: Exploring Common Ground

Hello [Name],

I admire your work in [Specific Area] and believe there's potential for collaboration. Let's connect and discuss how we can support each other's goals.

Best regards, [Your Name] [LinkedIn Profile]

Version 3: Personalized Approach

Subject: Connecting with Purpose

Dear [Name],

I read your recent article on [Topic] and found it insightful. Let's connect and explore synergies between our work. Looking forward to learning from each other.

Best regards, [Your Name] [LinkedIn Profile]

Follow-Up Email Templates

Version 1: Resource Sharing

Subject: Follow-Up: Our Conversation

Hi [Name],

Thank you for our recent chat. As promised, here's the [Resource/Article/Report] we discussed. I hope you find it valuable.

Best regards, [Your Name] [LinkedIn Profile]

Version 2: Gratitude and Next Steps

Subject: Grateful for Our Chat

Hi [Name],

I appreciate our conversation about [Topic]. Let's continue the dialogue. How about scheduling a follow-up call next week?

Best regards, [Your Name] [LinkedIn Profile]

Version 3: Reflecting on Insights

Subject: *Insights from Our Discussion*

Hi [Name],

Your perspective on [Topic] was enlightening. I've been reflecting on our chat. Let's keep the momentum going.

Best regards, [Your Name] [LinkedIn Profile]

Feel free to choose the templates that resonate with your networking style and adapt them to your specific context. Remember, personalization is key!

Assignments

- **Assignment 1**: Develop a networking strategy using AI tools, focusing on identifying and connecting with at least five key individuals.
- **Assignment 2**: Create and execute a one-month social media plan aimed at growing your professional network.
- **Assignment 3**: Engage in a real-world networking opportunity and document the process and outcomes.1

Assessment

- A quiz to assess understanding of AI's role in networking.
- Peer and instructor review of networking strategies and social media plans.

Module 3: AI for Career Development

Lesson 1: Embracing AI in Your Career

Understanding AI's Role: Exploring how AI is shaping careers across different industries.

In the ever-evolving landscape of the professional world, Artificial Intelligence (AI) has emerged as a transformative force, reshaping the contours of careers across a multitude of industries. As we delve into the third module of our course on AI for Career Development, it is imperative to understand the profound impact AI is having on the job market and how professionals can harness its potential for career advancement.

The Current Landscape of Work

The traditional job structures, once defined by routine and predictability, are undergoing a seismic shift due to the rapid advancement of AI technologies. The integration of AI into various sectors is not only optimizing tasks but also creating new roles and opportunities. The dichotomy between routine, rule-based tasks and those requiring creativity and complex problem-solving is becoming more pronounced, necessitating a workforce that is adaptable and skilled in leveraging AI.

AI in Specific Industries

Healthcare

In healthcare, AI is revolutionizing patient care with predictive analytics, personalized medicine, and robotic assistance in surgeries. It is enhancing the capabilities of healthcare professionals, allowing them to provide more accurate diagnoses and effective treatments.

Finance

The finance industry is witnessing a surge in AI-driven tools for risk assessment, fraud detection, and algorithmic trading. Professionals in this sector are now expected to possess a blend of financial expertise and technological acumen.

Manufacturing

AI-powered automation in manufacturing is increasing efficiency and productivity. From predictive maintenance to smart logistics, AI is enabling a new era of manufacturing that is more responsive and sustainable.

IT/Software Development

The IT and software development industries are at the forefront of AI innovation. AI is not only streamlining development processes but also creating a demand for new skills such as machine learning and AI ethics.

Embracing AI in Your Career

To thrive in this AI-infused job market, professionals must be proactive in embracing AI. This involves:

- **Upskilling and Reskilling**: Continuously learning new AI-related skills and technologies to stay competitive.
- **Adaptability**: Being open to change and ready to pivot into new roles that AI may create.
- **Collaboration**: Working alongside AI, leveraging its strengths to enhance human capabilities.

Lesson 2: AI-Driven Career Planning

Career Pathing with AI: Utilizing AI to map out potential career paths and opportunities.

In the second lesson of our module on AI for Career Development, we turn our attention to the innovative ways in which Artificial Intelligence (AI) can be employed to chart potential career trajectories and unearth new professional opportunities. The advent of AI has not only automated mundane tasks but also provided us with powerful tools to envision and navigate our future careers with unprecedented precision.

The Advent of Predictive Career Pathing

Predictive career pathing is an AI-driven approach that leverages historical data, industry trends, and personal performance metrics to forecast potential career progressions. This method illuminates possible future roles and delineates the skills and experiences required to attain them.

AI Tools for Career Pathing

AI-Powered Career Advisors

AI career advisors analyze your skills, experience, and preferences to suggest personalized career paths. They can provide insights into which industries or roles you are best suited for and what steps you need to take to get there.

Job Market Analysis

AI tools can scan the job market to identify emerging roles and sectors, giving you a competitive edge by preparing you for future demand. They can also suggest educational resources or certifications that will make you more attractive to employers.

Skill Gap Analysis

By comparing your current skill set with the requirements of your desired role, AI can highlight the gaps you need to fill. It can then recommend specific courses or learning materials to help you acquire the necessary skills.

Implementing AI in Your Career Strategy

To effectively utilize AI in career pathing, consider the following steps:

- *Assess Your Current Position*: Use AI to evaluate where you stand in your career and identify your strengths and weaknesses.
- *Explore AI-Generated Career Paths*: Engage with AI tools that suggest career trajectories based on your profile and goals.
- *Develop a Learning Plan*: Based on AI's recommendations, create a tailored plan to acquire new skills and knowledge.
- *Monitor Industry Trends*: Keep an eye on AI-generated reports about the latest industry trends and adjust your career path accordingly.
- *Helpful AI tools to complete this lesson:*
- *Resume.io*: An AI tool for resume building that offers customizable templates and automatic summarization to help create professional resumes.
- *JobScan*: This tool specializes in resume analysis and optimization, ensuring compatibility with Applicant Tracking Systems (ATS) and LinkedIn profile optimization.
- *Wizco*: Offers expert-led mock interviews and AI-powered interview coaching, providing post-session reports and actionable insights.
- *Zavvy*: An AI tool designed for human resources that facilitates AI-powered career pathing and data-driven development plans.
- *Career Copilot*: Provides personalized career path guidance, skill enhancement opportunities, and job market insights.
- *Coursera for Business*: An AI tool for learning and development that offers a wide range of courses tailored to career growth.

Activity: Create a personalized career development plan using AI-powered tools.

Objective:

To leverage AI tools to develop a tailored career development plan that aligns with your professional goals and aspirations.

Instructions:

1. **Self-Assessment**:
   - Use an AI tool like **Career Copilot** to assess your current skills, experience, and career interests.
   - Reflect on your strengths, weaknesses, and areas where AI suggests you could improve or learn new skills.
2. **Career Path Exploration**:
   - Explore AI-generated career paths with tools such as **Zavvy** or **Resume.io** to understand potential future roles and industries that align with your profile.
   - Identify the skills and qualifications required for the roles you are interested in.
3. **Skill Gap Analysis**:
   - Conduct a skill gap analysis using AI tools like **JobScan** to compare your current skill set with the requirements of your desired role.
   - List down the skills you need to develop or enhance.
4. **Learning Plan Creation**:
   - Based on the skill gap analysis, use AI tools such as **Coursera for Business** to find courses and certifications that will help you acquire the necessary skills.
   - Create a learning plan with specific goals, timelines, and resources.
5. **Networking Strategy**:
   - Utilize AI tools to identify networking opportunities and professional groups that can support your career development.
   - Plan to attend events, webinars, or online forums where you can connect with industry professionals.
6. **Performance Tracking**:
   - Set up a system to track your progress using AI tools that offer performance evaluations and feedback.
   - Regularly review your achievements and adjust your plan as needed.
7. **Mentorship and Coaching**:
   - Seek AI-powered mentorship and coaching recommendations to find professionals who can guide you on your career path.
   - Engage in mentorship programs or one-on-one coaching sessions to gain insights and advice.

Lesson 3: Building a Future-Proof Career

Adapting to AI Disruption: Strategies for staying relevant in an AI-transformed job market.

The advent of Artificial Intelligence (AI) has ushered in a new era of innovation and disruption, significantly altering the job market landscape. As AI continues to advance, it is imperative for professionals to develop strategies to adapt and remain relevant. This lesson explores practical approaches to ensure career longevity in the face of AI disruption.

Understanding the Impact of AI

Before we can adapt, we must first understand the dual nature of AI's impact on the job market:

- **Job Creation**: AI has led to the emergence of new roles such as AI specialists, data scientists, and ethics compliance managers.
- **Job Displacement**: Routine and rule-based jobs are at risk of being automated, particularly in sectors like manufacturing and transportation.

Strategies for Adapting to AI

Lifelong Learning

Embrace continuous education to stay current with the latest AI advancements and related skills.

Skill Diversification

Develop a broad skill set that includes both technical and soft skills. Focus on areas like analytical thinking, creative problem-solving, and leadership'.

Embracing Change

Cultivate a mindset that welcomes change and innovation. Be prepared to pivot into new roles and industries that AI may create.

Here are a list of examples of AI roles that can be replaced and created by AI in the near future to consider on you work.

Traditional Roles Replaced or Improved by AI:

1. **Supply Chain Optimization**: AI is increasingly used to automate and optimize supply chain processes.
2. **Legal Research**: AI can perform legal research tasks, reducing the time lawyers spend on case preparation.
3. **Financial Analysis**: AI tools can analyze financial data more quickly and accurately than humans.
4. **Predictive Maintenance**: AI can predict when machines will need maintenance, reducing downtime in manufacturing.

5. **Telemarketing**: AI-powered systems can handle sales calls and customer inquiries, potentially replacing human telemarketers.
6. **Bookkeeping Clerks**: AI can manage financial records and transactions with high accuracy.
7. **Receptionists**: AI chatbots can schedule appointments and handle customer service tasks.
8. **Couriers**: Autonomous delivery vehicles and drones are beginning to replace traditional courier services.
9. **Market Research Analysts**: AI can analyze market trends and consumer behavior more efficiently.
10. **Retail Salespeople**: AI can provide customer service and sales assistance online, reducing the need for in-store staff.

New Roles Created by AI:

1. **AI Trainer and Operator**: Professionals who train AI systems and ensure they operate correctly.
2. **Sentiment Analyzer**: Experts who use AI to interpret and act on customer feedback.
3. **AI-Generated Work Auditor**: Individuals responsible for auditing AI-generated content.
4. **AI Prediction Analyzer**: Specialists who interpret AI-generated predictions for strategic decision-making.
5. **AI Input and Output Manager**: Managers who oversee the data inputs and outputs of AI systems.
6. **AI Integration Specialist**: Professionals who integrate AI technologies into business processes.
7. **AI Compliance Manager**: Experts who ensure AI applications comply with regulations.
8. **AI Healthcare Diagnostician**: Medical professionals who use AI for diagnostics.
9. **AI Ethicist**: Individuals focusing on the ethical implications of AI.
10. **Content Creator**: Creative roles that provide input for AI learning and content generation.

These examples illustrate how AI is reshaping the workforce, creating opportunities for new roles while enhancing or replacing traditional ones. As AI continues to evolve, we can expect further changes in the job market landscape.

Ethical Considerations

Understand the ethical implications of AI and strive to implement AI solutions responsibly.

Networking

Engage with professional communities to share knowledge and stay informed about AI trends and opportunities.

Conclusion

Adapting to AI disruption requires a proactive approach to career development. By understanding AI's impact, continuously learning, diversifying skills, embracing change, and networking, professionals can not only survive but thrive in an AI-transformed job market.

Innovation and Entrepreneurship: Harnessing AI for creating new business opportunities.

In the realm of entrepreneurship, innovation is the cornerstone of growth and success. With the advent of Artificial Intelligence (AI), a new horizon of business opportunities has emerged, offering entrepreneurs the tools to innovate, disrupt, and lead in their respective industries. This lesson explores how AI can be harnessed to create new business opportunities and drive entrepreneurial ventures.

The AI Advantage in Entrepreneurship

AI technology offers a competitive edge in several key areas:

- **Automation and Efficiency**: AI can automate complex processes, allowing businesses to operate more efficiently and at a lower cost.
- **Data Analysis and Decision-Making**: Entrepreneurs can use AI to analyze vast amounts of data, gaining insights that inform strategic decisions.
- **Personalization and Customer Engagement**: AI enables businesses to offer personalized experiences, enhancing customer satisfaction and loyalty.

Identifying AI-Driven Opportunities

To identify opportunities where AI can be leveraged, entrepreneurs should:

- **Assess Market Needs**: Look for gaps in the market where AI can provide a solution or enhance existing products and services.
- **Stay Informed**: Keep abreast of the latest AI developments and trends to anticipate new business opportunities.
- **Engage with AI Communities**: Participate in AI forums and networks to exchange ideas and collaborate on innovative projects.

Strategies for Harnessing AI

- **Pilot Projects**: Test AI technologies in small-scale projects to understand their potential impact and refine your approach.
- **Collaboration**: Partner with AI experts and technology providers to develop unique solutions tailored to your business needs.
- **Invest in AI Skills**: Build a team with AI expertise or invest in training to develop the necessary skills within your organization.

Case Studies of AI-Driven Success

- *AI in Retail*: Companies using AI for inventory management, customer behavior prediction, and personalized marketing campaigns.
- *AI in Healthcare*: Startups leveraging AI for diagnostic tools, treatment personalization, and patient care optimization.
- *AI in Finance*: Fintech firms employing AI for credit scoring, fraud detection, and automated financial advising.

Conclusion

Harnessing AI for creating new business opportunities requires a blend of entrepreneurial spirit, strategic thinking, and technological savvy. By embracing AI, entrepreneurs can unlock innovative pathways, redefine industries, and establish themselves as leaders in the new business landscape.

Activity: Develop a proposal for an AI-related project or business idea.

Objective:

To create a proposal for an AI-related project or business idea that focuses on adapting to AI disruption in the job market and harnessing AI for innovation and entrepreneurship.

Instructions:

1. **Identify a Market Need**:
   - Reflect on the discussions from the previous lessons about AI's impact on careers and business opportunities.
   - Choose a specific industry or job function that is undergoing significant changes due to AI.
2. **Define Your AI Solution**:
   - Propose an AI tool or service that helps professionals adapt to changes in their field or helps businesses capitalize on new opportunities created by AI.
   - Explain how your solution will address the identified market need and what makes it innovative.
3. **Market Analysis**:
   - Conduct a market analysis to understand the demand for your solution.
   - Identify your target audience and potential competitors.
4. **Business Model**:
   - Outline how your project or business will generate revenue.
   - Discuss pricing, cost structure, and potential funding sources.
5. **Implementation Plan**:
   - Create a step-by-step plan for developing and launching your AI solution.
   - Include milestones, timelines, and required resources.
6. **Impact Assessment**:
   - Evaluate the potential impact of your solution on the job market and in fostering entrepreneurship.

- Discuss how it will help individuals and businesses adapt to and thrive in an AI-transformed landscape.

Deliverable:

A detailed proposal document that includes the following sections:

- Executive Summary
- Introduction to the Market Need
- Description of the AI Solution
- Market Analysis
- Business Model
- Implementation Plan
- Impact Assessment
- Conclusion

Outcome:

By completing this activity, you will have a structured proposal for an AI-related project or business idea that is ready to be presented to stakeholders, investors, or partners

Resources – Module 3

- Guides on using AI for career planning and upskilling.

Guide 1: AI for Career Planning

Step 1: Self-Assessment

- Use AI Tools: Leverage AI-powered career assessment tools to evaluate your strengths, weaknesses, and interests.
- Identify Career Goals: Define what you want to achieve in your career and set short-term and long-term goals.

Step 2: Market Research

- AI-Driven Job Market Analysis: Utilize AI to analyze job trends and identify growing fields and opportunities.
- Skill Demand Identification: Determine which skills are in high demand in your chosen field.

Step 3: Pathway Planning

- AI Career Path Suggestions: Explore AI-generated career paths based on your profile and goals.
- Milestone Setting: Use AI to set realistic milestones and timelines for achieving your career objectives.

Step 4: Networking

- AI-Enhanced Networking: Engage with AI-powered networking platforms to connect with industry professionals and mentors.

Step 5: Continuous Learning

- AI-Curated Learning: Enroll in AI-recommended courses and certifications to acquire the necessary skills.
- Skill Tracking: Keep track of your skill development with AI tools that monitor learning progress.

Guide 2: AI for Upskilling

Step 1: Skill Gap Analysis

- AI Skill Assessment: Use AI to analyze your current skills and compare them with industry requirements.
- Identify Upskilling Needs: Pinpoint the areas where you need improvement or new skills.

Step 2: Learning Plan Development

- AI-Personalized Courses: Find AI-suggested courses tailored to your upskilling needs.
- Schedule Creation: Develop a learning schedule with AI assistance to ensure consistent progress.

Step 3: Hands-On Practice

- AI Simulations: Participate in AI-driven simulations and projects to apply new skills in real-world scenarios.
- Project Feedback: Get AI-generated feedback on your projects to refine your skills further.

Step 4: Certification

- **AI-Validated Credentials**: Obtain certifications for new skills with AI verification to add credibility to your resume.
- **Digital Portfolio**: Build a digital portfolio of your work and certifications using AI tools.

Step 5: Application

- **AI Job Matching**: Match your new skills with job opportunities using AI job search platforms.
- **Interview Preparation**: Prepare for interviews with AI-powered interview coaching and practice sessions.

Assignments

- *Assignment 1*: Conduct a self-assessment of AI skills and create an upskilling action plan.
- *Assignment 2*: Utilize an AI career pathing tool to explore and document potential career moves.
- *Assignment 3*: Engage with an AI mentorship platform and summarize the insights gained.

Assessment

- A quiz to test the participants' understanding of AI's impact on career development.

Module 4: Productivity and Time Management

Welcome to Module 4: Productivity and Time Management. As we continue our journey through the transformative world of AI and its applications in professional development, we now turn our focus to one of the most crucial aspects of career success: managing our time effectively.

In this module, we will explore how AI tools can significantly enhance our productivity by optimizing our schedules, streamlining task management, and improving our ability to prioritize. As a career development specialist, I will guide you through the latest AI applications that are designed to boost your efficiency and help you manage your time like never before.

Let's embark on this journey to unlock the full potential of AI in elevating your productivity and time management skills.

Lesson 1: AI for Personal Efficiency

Time Management Tools: Explore AI applications for scheduling, task management, and prioritization.

In today's fast-paced world, effective time management is not just a desirable skill but a necessity. AI has stepped in as a powerful ally, offering a suite of applications that can transform how we organize our day-to-day activities. Let's explore some of the AI applications that are at the forefront of scheduling, task management, and prioritization:

- **AI Scheduling Assistants**: These tools take over the tedious task of managing your calendar. They can schedule meetings, avoid conflicts, and even reschedule appointments when emergencies arise.
- **AI Task Managers**: With the ability to learn from your habits, AI task managers prioritize your tasks based on urgency and importance, helping you focus on what matters most.
- **AI Project Management**: For those juggling multiple projects, AI-assisted project management tools can predict timelines, allocate resources efficiently, and keep your projects on track.

By leveraging these AI tools, you can ensure that your time is used effectively, leading to increased productivity and a more balanced professional life. In the following sections, we will delve deeper into each of these applications, providing you with the knowledge to choose the right tools for your needs and integrate them seamlessly into your workflow.

Prioritization Strategies: Use AI to identify high-impact tasks and allocate time effectively.

In the pursuit of personal efficiency, the ability to prioritize tasks is paramount. AI has the power to transform this critical aspect of time management by helping us identify high-impact tasks and allocate our time more effectively. Here's how AI can be leveraged for superior prioritization:

- **AI Maturity Assessment**: Begin by evaluating your or your team's AI maturity level. This will inform the selection of AI tools that are best suited to your current capabilities.
- **Quick Wins vs. Big Wins**: AI can help categorize tasks into 'quick wins' that offer immediate value with minimal effort and 'big wins' that require more investment but promise significant long-term benefits.
- **Risk-Reward Analysis**: Utilize AI to conduct a structured risk-reward analysis, quantifying the viability of tasks and ensuring that you focus on those with the highest potential impact1.
- **AI Task Prioritization Tools**: Implement AI-driven task prioritization tools that automate the sorting and ranking of tasks based on urgency, importance, and impact. This helps in making informed decisions about what to focus on and when.
- **AI Prioritization Matrix**: Employ an AI-powered prioritization matrix generator to create a custom matrix that aids in visualizing and deciding on task priority .

By integrating these AI-driven strategies into your workflow, you can ensure that your efforts are concentrated on tasks that drive the most value, thereby enhancing your productivity and achieving your goals more efficiently. AI not only simplifies the process of prioritization but also adds a layer of data-driven decision-making that can significantly boost personal and team performance.

Activity: Implement an AI-based time management tool for a week and reflect on the experience.

Here are some of examples of tools to be used to complete this activity.

1. **TimeTo**: An AI platform that prioritizes focus time and optimizes schedules to increase productivity.
2. **Timely**: An AI-powered time tracking software that accurately tracks time for projects and integrates with popular apps.
3. **Clockwise**: Optimizes your calendar to create blocks of uninterrupted time, improving focus and productivity.
4. **FlowSavvy**: A tool designed to manage workflows and tasks efficiently using AI.
5. **FocusDoro**: Combines AI with the Pomodoro technique to help you stay focused on tasks.
6. **SkedPal**: An AI scheduler that plans your tasks based on your priorities and available time.
7. **timeOS AI**: Offers a smart way to manage your time with AI-driven insights and suggestions.
8. **Reclaim AI**: Helps in intelligently scheduling time for work and personal life balance.

Lesson 2: Overcoming Procrastination

Procrastination is the silent thief of time, stealthily eroding our most valuable resource with the promise of tomorrow. Yet, in the professional realm, where deadlines shape our days and productivity is the benchmark of success, succumbing to procrastination can be the Achilles' heel of career advancement. In this pivotal Module 4, Lesson 2, we delve into the art of overcoming procrastination, not just with fleeting tactics, but with a transformative approach that aligns with the very essence of our course—leveraging AI for career development.

The Psychology Behind Procrastination

Understanding procrastination requires a deep dive into the psychological undercurrents that drive this behavior. It's not merely a lapse in time management; it's an emotional response to tasks that evoke discomfort—be it anxiety, self-doubt, or fear of failure. The irony lies in the fact that avoidance brings temporary relief but culminates in heightened stress and diminished self-esteem.

AI as Your Ally Against Procrastination

In the age of AI, we have the unprecedented advantage of harnessing technology to combat procrastination. AI-driven tools can dissect our schedules, analyze our work patterns, and nudge us towards efficiency with personalized reminders and motivational insights. They serve as virtual coaches, guiding us through the labyrinth of our to-do lists with precision and foresight.

AI-Enhanced Time Management Tools

Imagine a suite of AI applications that not only schedules your tasks but also predicts future time blocks where productivity peaks. These tools adapt to your working style, learning from your habits to suggest optimal periods for deep work and creative endeavors.

Prioritization Through AI Analytics

AI doesn't just organize; it prioritizes. By analyzing the impact and urgency of your tasks, AI applications can create a hierarchy of activities, ensuring that your focus remains on high-value tasks that propel you towards your goals.

The Role of AI in Habit Formation

Consistency is key in overcoming procrastination, and AI can be instrumental in forming productive habits. Through pattern recognition and reinforcement learning, AI tools can craft personalized habit-building programs, turning productivity into a natural part of your daily routine.

A Step-by-Step Guide to Overcoming Procrastination with AI

1. **Identify Procrastination Triggers**: Use AI to monitor your activity and pinpoint moments of procrastination. Awareness is the first step towards change.
2. **Set AI-Driven Goals**: Establish clear, measurable goals using AI tools that can track your progress and adjust your objectives in real-time.
3. **Embrace AI-Recommended Micro-Tasks**: Break down overwhelming projects into smaller, AI-recommended tasks that are manageable and less intimidating.

4. **Engage with AI-Powered Motivation**: Receive AI-generated encouragement and rewards for completing tasks, tapping into the power of positive reinforcement.

5. **Reflect with AI**: Utilize AI to reflect on your productivity patterns, learn from past behaviors, and strategize for future success.

Conclusion

Overcoming procrastination is not about finding more hours in the day; it's about making each hour count. With AI as your strategic partner, you can transform procrastination into productivity, turning the tide in your favor. As we continue to explore the vast potential of AI in career development, let this lesson be a testament to the power of technology in unlocking human potential and fostering a culture of relentless progress.

In the next lesson, we will build upon these foundations, exploring advanced AI techniques for time management and productivity. Together, we will journey towards a future where procrastination is a relic of the past, and peak productivity is the new norm.

- **AI for Goal Setting**: Set and track long-term goals with AI assistance.
- **Activity**: Create a goal-setting plan using an AI tool and outline steps for ongoing tracking.

Bonus Module: Enhancing Your Resume with AI

Lesson 1: Introduction to AI Resume Tools

Overview of AI in Resumes: Understanding how AI can optimize your resume.

In today's competitive job market, standing out is more important than ever. With the advent of Artificial Intelligence (AI), candidates now have a powerful ally in crafting resumes that not only highlight their skills and experiences but also align perfectly with what employers are looking for.

AI-powered resume tools are designed to optimize your resume by analyzing job descriptions and industry trends to suggest the most relevant keywords and phrases. These tools go beyond simple spell-checking and formatting; they provide strategic insights that can elevate your resume from good to great.

Here's how AI can enhance your resume:

- **Keyword Optimization**: AI tools can scan job listings to identify essential keywords and suggest where to include them in your resume, ensuring it passes through Applicant Tracking Systems (ATS) with ease.
- **Tailored Content**: By understanding the nuances of job descriptions, AI can help tailor your resume content to match the specific requirements of each role you apply for.
- **Formatting and Structure**: AI can suggest the most effective resume layouts and structures, emphasizing your strengths and ensuring a clean, professional appearance.
- **Performance Metrics**: Some AI tools can even provide feedback on how your resume performs in real-time, allowing for continuous improvement.

By leveraging AI, you can ensure that your resume is not only a reflection of your professional journey but also a strategic tool that increases your chances of landing your dream job.

- **Selecting the Right AI Tools**: Reviewing different AI resume builders and enhancers.

When it comes to enhancing your resume with AI, selecting the right tools is crucial. With a plethora of AI resume builders and enhancers available, it's important to choose one that aligns with your career goals and industry requirements. Here's a guide to help you navigate the options and select the best AI resume tool for your needs.

1. Understanding AI Resume Builders

AI resume builders are more than just templates; they are sophisticated platforms that use machine learning algorithms to tailor your resume. They analyze job descriptions, identify key skills and phrases, and optimize your resume to increase your chances of passing through Applicant Tracking Systems (ATS).

2. Features to Look For

When reviewing AI resume builders, consider the following features:

- **Keyword Optimization**: The tool should offer keyword suggestions that match your industry and the jobs you're targeting.
- **Customization Options**: Look for builders that allow you to customize sections, layouts, and designs to fit your personal brand.
- **Feedback and Scoring**: Some tools provide scores based on how well your resume matches job descriptions, which can be invaluable feedback.
- **Integration with Job Boards**: The best tools can directly parse job listings from popular job boards and suggest optimizations.

3. Top AI Resume Builders

Based on recent reviews, here are some of the top AI resume builders to consider:

- *ResumeLab: Known for a wide range of templates and a user-friendly interface, ResumeLab also offers detailed guides on resume writing.*
- *Rezi.ai: This tool focuses on creating ATS-optimized resumes and provides real-time content analysis to improve your resume's effectiveness.*
- *Zety: Zety is praised for its intuitive design and comprehensive job application tools, including cover letter builders and resume checks.*

4. Making the Choice

To select the right AI resume builder, start by identifying your specific needs. Are you looking for a tool that offers in-depth content analysis, or do you prioritize design and customization? Consider trying out a few options to see which one you're most comfortable with and which yields the best results for your resume.

Remember, the goal of using an AI resume builder is not just to create a visually appealing resume but to craft a strategic document that resonates with recruiters and hiring managers in your field

Activity: Explore and compare various AI resume tools.

Objective:

To understand the strengths and weaknesses of different AI resume tools and determine which one best suit your individual needs for enhancing your resume.

Instructions:

1. **Research Phase**:
   - Begin by researching the following AI resume builders: **KickResume, Rezi, Resume.io, ResuMaker AI, TealHQ,** and **ResumAI**.

- Visit each tool's website and note down the key features they offer. Pay special attention to keyword optimization, customization options, feedback mechanisms, and integration with job boards.
2. **Comparison Chart Creation**:
   - Create a comparison chart with the following columns: Tool Name, Keyword Optimization, Customization, Feedback & Scoring, Job Board Integration, and Overall User Experience.
   - Fill in the chart based on the information gathered during your research.
3. **Practical Exploration**:
   - Select two AI resume tools from your research that you find most promising.
   - Use each tool to create or enhance your resume. If possible, use the same content for both to have a direct comparison.
4. **Analysis and Reflection**:
   - Analyze the resumes generated by each tool. Consider the following questions:
     - How did each tool handle keyword optimization?
     - Were the customization options sufficient and easy to use?
     - What kind of feedback did the tool provide, and was it helpful?
     - Did the tool offer any unique features that stood out to you?
5. **Report Writing**:
   - Write a report summarizing your findings. Include your comparison chart and a brief review of each tool you explored.
   - Conclude with a recommendation for the best AI resume tool based on your experience and its suitability for different types of job seekers.

Deliverables:

- A completed comparison chart.
- A written report with your analysis and recommendations.

Reflection:

After completing this activity, reflect on how AI can be a powerful ally in career development. Discuss how the right AI tool can make a significant difference in how a resume is perceived by potential employers

Lesson 2: Analyzing Your Current Resume with AI

AI Resume Analysis: Using AI to identify strengths and weaknesses in your current resume.

In the realm of career development, AI has emerged as a pivotal tool for analyzing and enhancing resumes. AI resume analysis tools are adept at dissecting the intricate details of your resume, providing insights into its strengths and pinpointing areas that require improvement.

How AI Analyzes Resumes

AI resume analysis tools employ sophisticated algorithms to evaluate various aspects of your resume. Here's what they typically assess:

- **Impact**: AI tools scrutinize the effectiveness of your language, ensuring that your achievements are communicated powerfully and concisely.
- **Brevity**: They analyze the length of your resume and bullet points, suggesting edits to make your content more succinct.
- **Consistency**: These tools check for uniformity in your resume's formatting and style, which is crucial for a professional appearance.
- **Keyword Relevance**: AI compares your resume against job descriptions to recommend the most pertinent keywords and phrases, enhancing your resume's visibility to recruiters.

Benefits of AI Resume Analysis

Utilizing AI for resume analysis can provide several advantages:

- **Objective Evaluation**: AI offers an unbiased assessment of your resume, free from human error or subjective judgment.
- **Tailored Suggestions**: You receive personalized recommendations based on industry standards and job-specific criteria.
- **Real-Time Feedback**: Instant feedback allows for quick iterations and improvements to your resume.
- **Competitive Edge**: By aligning your resume with what recruiters are searching for, AI tools give you a competitive advantage in the job market.

Engaging with AI Resume Analysis

To fully leverage AI in analyzing your resume, consider the following steps:

1. **Choose a Reputable AI Resume Analysis Tool**: Select from top-rated options like Resume Worded or Enhancv, which are known for their comprehensive analysis capabilities.
2. **Upload Your Current Resume**: Provide your resume to the chosen AI tool for analysis.
3. **Review the AI's Feedback**: Examine the AI's critique and note the suggested improvements.
4. **Implement Changes**: Apply the AI's recommendations to enhance your resume.
5. **Iterate as Needed**: Repeat the process with updated versions of your resume to refine it further.

By integrating AI resume analysis into your career development strategy, you can ensure that your resume not only reflects your qualifications but also resonates with the evolving demands of the job market.

- **Keyword Optimization**: Learning how AI suggests industry-specific keywords and phrases.

In the digital age, where resumes often first encounter algorithms before human eyes, keyword optimization is essential. AI plays a pivotal role in ensuring your resume speaks the language of these algorithms, increasing your visibility to potential employers.

The Role of AI in Keyword Optimization

AI tools are adept at parsing job descriptions and identifying industry-specific keywords and phrases that are critical for your resume to pass through Applicant Tracking Systems (ATS). Here's how AI enhances keyword optimization:

- **Industry-Specific Tailoring**: AI analyzes job postings within your field to determine the most sought-after skills and terms, ensuring your resume aligns with industry expectations.
- **Relevance Scoring**: Some AI tools score your resume against job descriptions, highlighting the keywords you've matched and suggesting additions for those you've missed.
- **Semantic Matching**: Beyond exact keywords, AI can suggest synonyms and related terms that broaden your resume's appeal without keyword stuffing.

Benefits of AI-Driven Keyword Optimization

Leveraging AI for keyword optimization offers several benefits:

- **Increased ATS Compatibility**: By including the right keywords, AI ensures your resume is more likely to be shortlisted by ATS systems.
- **Enhanced Relevance**: AI helps maintain the relevance of your resume for the roles you're targeting, making it more attractive to recruiters.
- **Dynamic Adaptation**: As job market trends evolve, AI tools update their databases, keeping your resume current with the latest industry keywords.

Engaging with AI for Keyword Optimization

To effectively use AI for keyword optimization, consider the following steps:

1. **Select an AI Keyword Tool**: Choose a tool like Jobscan or Postlander, which are known for their robust keyword analysis features.
2. **Input Your Resume and Job Descriptions**: Provide your current resume and a few job descriptions you're interested in.
3. **Analyze the AI's Suggestions**: Review the keywords and phrases the AI tool recommends, noting any gaps in your current resume.
4. **Implement the Recommendations**: Integrate the suggested keywords into your resume, ensuring they fit naturally within the context.

5. **Iterate and Update**: Regularly update your resume with new keywords as you apply for different positions and as industry trends shift.

By incorporating AI-driven keyword optimization into your resume strategy, you can significantly enhance your resume's effectiveness and ensure it resonates with both ATS and human recruiters.

The Impact of Visual Elements in Resumes

First Impressions Matter

Visual elements in a resume are crucial for making a strong first impression. Studies have shown that hiring managers often make initial judgments within a few seconds of viewing a resume. Therefore, a visually appealing resume can capture attention and make your application memorable.

Visual Elements Enhance Readability

The strategic use of visual elements such as bullet points, bold text, and color can guide the reader's eye to the most important information. This enhances the readability of your resume and ensures that your key achievements and skills stand out.

Infographics and Data Visualization

For professions where data analysis and results are paramount, infographics and other visual data representations can quickly convey complex information. This not only showcases your skills but also demonstrates your ability to present data effectively.

Reflecting Your Personal Brand

Visual elements can also reflect your personal brand. The design choices you make—like color schemes and typography—can give insights into your personality and professional style.

Industry-Specific Expectations

In creative industries, such as graphic design or marketing, the expectation for visually striking resumes is higher. Here, your resume serves as a direct example of your design skills and creativity.

Balancing Content and Design

While visual elements are important, they should not overshadow the content. The most successful visual resumes strike a balance, leading the hiring manager to the most important aspects of your application without distracting from the content.

Adapting to Trends

As we spend more time on digital devices, our brains are becoming conditioned to process visuals more readily than blocks of text. A movement towards more visual resume styles has been gaining momentum, making it an increasingly important aspect to consider.

Activity: Run your resume through an AI analysis tool and note the feedback.

Lesson 3: Rewriting and Refining with AI

AI-Assisted Rewriting: Implementing AI suggestions to improve phrasing and impact.

The power of language lies in its ability to persuade, inform, and engage. In the professional world, the way you phrase your experiences and skills can make a significant difference. AI-assisted rewriting tools are designed to refine your language, ensuring that your resume communicates your value effectively.

How AI Enhances Resume Phrasing

AI rewriting tools use natural language processing (NLP) to analyze and suggest improvements to your resume's text. Here's what they typically focus on:

- **Clarity**: AI suggests simplifying complex sentences, making your resume more understandable.
- **Conciseness**: It helps eliminate redundancy, ensuring your points are made succinctly.
- **Impact**: AI identifies weak verbs and suggests more dynamic ones, adding strength to your achievements.
- **Tone**: The tools can adjust the tone to match the desired level of formality or industry standards.

Benefits of AI-Assisted Rewriting

Utilizing AI for rewriting offers several advantages:

- **Objective Feedback**: AI provides unbiased suggestions based on data-driven analysis.
- **Time Efficiency**: It significantly reduces the time spent on editing and refining text.
- **Consistency**: AI ensures consistent use of terminology and style throughout the resume.
- **Personalization**: Some AI tools can tailor suggestions based on the specific job you're applying for, increasing relevance.

Engaging with AI-Assisted Rewriting

To effectively use AI for rewriting and refining your resume, consider the following steps:

1. **Select a Reputable AI Rewriting Tool**: Options like QuillBot and Wordtune are known for their robust rewriting capabilities.
2. **Input Your Resume Text**: Provide sections of your resume to the AI tool for analysis.

3. **Review AI Suggestions**: Carefully consider the AI's recommendations and decide which ones to implement.
4. **Apply Changes**: Integrate the AI's suggestions into your resume, enhancing its overall quality.
5. **Iterate as Needed**: Repeat the process with updated versions of your resume to continuously improve its impact.

By incorporating AI-assisted rewriting into your resume refinement process, you can ensure that your document is not only well-written but also has the impact and clarity needed to stand out in the job market.

> Formatting for Success: Understanding how AI can suggest effective resume layouts.

The layout of your resume is just as important as the content. An effective layout ensures that your qualifications and achievements are presented in a clear, logical, and visually appealing manner. AI has revolutionized the way we approach resume formatting by offering data-backed suggestions tailored to your career field and experience level.

How AI Influences Resume Formatting

AI resume builders analyze successful resumes across various industries to determine the most effective layouts. They consider factors such as readability, ATS compatibility, and visual hierarchy. Here's how AI can guide you in formatting your resume for success:

- **Template Selection**: AI suggests templates that are both visually appealing and professional, suitable for your industry and experience level[1].
- **Section Organization**: It recommends the best way to organize your resume sections, ensuring that the most critical information catches the reader's eye first[2].
- **Visual Balance**: AI tools help maintain a balance between text and white space, making your resume easier to read and more attractive[3].

Benefits of AI-Suggested Layouts

Using AI to suggest resume layouts offers several benefits:

- **Personalization**: AI tools provide personalized layout suggestions based on your specific career goals and the roles you're targeting[4].
- **Efficiency**: They save time by automating the formatting process, allowing you to focus on fine-tuning your resume's content[5].
- **Adaptability**: AI resume builders are updated with the latest trends, ensuring your resume format stays current and competitive[1].

Engaging with AI for Resume Formatting

To utilize AI for effective resume formatting, consider the following steps:

1. **Choose an AI Resume Builder**: Select a tool like Resume Genius or Canva, which are known for their extensive template libraries and formatting suggestions.
2. **Input Your Information**: Provide details about your education, experience, and the job you're applying for.
3. **Review AI Suggestions**: Examine the layout options presented by the AI and choose the one that best represents your professional image.
4. **Customize as Needed**: While AI provides a strong starting point, don't hesitate to make adjustments that reflect your personal brand.
5. **Iterate and Update**: As you gain more experience or target new roles, revisit the AI tool to update your resume's layout accordingly.

By leveraging AI for resume formatting, you can create a document that not only showcases your qualifications but also does so in a way that is both aesthetically pleasing and aligned with industry standards.

Lesson 4: Tailoring Your Resume for the Job

Job Description Analysis: Leveraging AI to tailor your resume to specific job postings.

In the quest for your ideal job, tailoring your resume to each specific job posting can significantly increase your chances of landing an interview. AI tools are particularly adept at analyzing job descriptions and helping you customize your resume accordingly.

How AI Facilitates Job Description Analysis

AI-powered job analysis tools can dissect a job description to identify key knowledge, skills, and abilities (KSAs) required for the role. Here's how they assist in tailoring your resume:

- **Keyword Extraction**: AI tools extract essential keywords and phrases from the job description that should be mirrored in your resume.
- **Skill Matching**: They compare your current resume against the job description to suggest which of your skills and experiences to highlight.
- **Gap Identification**: AI identifies any gaps between your resume and the job requirements, allowing you to address them proactively.

Engaging with AI for Job Description Analysis

To leverage AI in tailoring your resume, follow these steps:

1. **Select an AI Job Analysis Tool**: Choose a tool that specializes in job description analysis, such as Wonderlic AI or others mentioned in the search results.
2. **Input the Job Description**: Provide the job description to the AI tool.
3. **Analyze AI Feedback**: Review the AI's analysis, noting the keywords and skills it identifies as crucial for the role.
4. **Tailor Your Resume**: Update your resume to include the AI's suggestions, ensuring it aligns closely with the job description.
5. **Iterate for Each Application**: Repeat this process for each job you apply for, customizing your resume to match each unique job description.

By using AI to analyze job descriptions, you can create a highly targeted resume that speaks directly to the needs of employers, thereby increasing your visibility and the likelihood of securing an interview.

Competitive Edge: How AI compares your resume to others in the field.

Gaining a competitive edge in the job market often requires understanding how your resume stacks up against others. AI tools can provide this insight by comparing your resume to a wide range of resumes in your field.

How AI Compares Resumes

AI resume builders and comparison tools analyze large datasets of resumes to determine what makes a resume successful in your industry. Here's what they offer:

- **Benchmarking**: AI tools benchmark your resume against others, highlighting areas where your resume excels or falls short.
- **Success Metrics**: They provide metrics on how well your resume aligns with industry standards and successful resumes.
- **Recommendations for Improvement**: Based on the comparison, AI suggests improvements to help your resume stand out.

Engaging with AI for Resume Comparison

To use AI for gaining a competitive edge, follow these steps:

1. **Choose an AI Resume Comparison Tool**: Select from top AI resume builders like Resume Genius, Rezi, or Kickresume, which offer comparison features.
2. **Input Your Resume**: Provide your resume to the AI tool.
3. **Review Comparative Analysis**: Examine the AI's comparison of your resume to others in your field.
4. **Implement AI Suggestions**: Use the AI's recommendations to refine your resume, focusing on areas that will give you a competitive advantage.
5. **Continuous Improvement**: As you gain more experience or the job market evolves, use AI tools to reassess your resume and make necessary updates.

Utilizing AI for resume comparison can provide you with valuable insights into how to differentiate your resume and highlight your unique strengths, giving you an edge over other candidates in your industry.

Lesson 5: Finalizing Your AI-Enhanced Resume

Error Checking: Utilizing AI for grammar and consistency checks.

Before sending out your resume, it's crucial to ensure it's free of errors. AI tools are invaluable for conducting thorough grammar and consistency checks, ensuring your resume is polished and professional.

How AI Tools Help with Error Checking

AI-powered grammar checkers can detect a wide range of errors, from simple typos to complex grammatical issues. They also ensure consistency in your use of language, formatting, and style across the entire document. Here's what they offer:

- **Comprehensive Grammar Review**: AI tools like Wordvice AI and Trinka go beyond basic spell checking to provide advanced grammar corrections.
- **Style and Tone Adjustments**: They suggest improvements to match the formal tone expected in a resume and maintain consistency throughout.

- **Real-Time Corrections**: As you make edits, AI tools provide immediate feedback, allowing for a streamlined revision process.

Engaging with AI for Error Checking

To utilize AI for error checking, follow these steps:

1. **Select an AI Grammar Checker**: Choose from tools like Wordvice AI, Trinka, or Grammarly, which are known for their comprehensive error-checking capabilities.
2. **Input Your Resume Text**: Run your resume text through the AI tool.
3. **Review AI Feedback**: Carefully consider the AI's suggestions for corrections and improvements.
4. **Apply Changes**: Make the necessary edits to your resume based on the AI's recommendations.
5. **Final Review**: Conduct a final review to ensure all changes have been implemented and no new errors have been introduced.

By incorporating AI grammar and consistency checks, you can present a resume that is error-free and reflects a high level of attention to detail.

AI Review and Feedback: Getting a final critique from an AI tool.

Once you've made all the necessary revisions to your resume, getting a final critique from an AI tool can provide valuable insights. AI review tools can simulate the perspective of a recruiter, giving you feedback on how your resume might be perceived.

How AI Tools Provide Final Reviews

AI resume review tools analyze your resume in the context of industry standards and successful resumes in your field. They provide scores and detailed feedback on various aspects of your resume. Here's how they assist in the final review:

- **Resume Scoring**: Tools like Kickresume and Resume Worded score your resume based on criteria such as content, structure, and impact.
- **Benchmarking**: They compare your resume to a database of successful resumes, highlighting areas of strength and those needing improvement.
- **Personalized Feedback**: AI tools offer tailored suggestions for enhancing your resume's effectiveness.

Engaging with AI for Final Review and Feedback

To get a final critique from an AI tool, follow these steps:

1. **Choose an AI Resume Review Tool**: Select a tool like Kickresume or Resume Worded, which provides detailed resume critiques.
2. **Upload Your Resume**: Provide your finalized resume to the AI tool.
3. **Analyze AI Feedback**: Review the detailed analysis and scores given by the AI.
4. **Implement Final Edits**: Use the AI's feedback to make any last-minute adjustments to your resume.

5. **Confidence in Submission**: With the AI's final critique, you can submit your resume with confidence, knowing it has been thoroughly reviewed.

Utilizing AI for a final review ensures that your resume is not only free of errors but also optimized to make a strong impression on potential employers.

Activity: Perform a final polish of your resume with an AI tool and prepare it for submission.

Resources

- A curated list of AI resume enhancement tools.
- Guides on interpreting AI feedback and implementing suggestions.

Assignments

- **Assignment 1**: Conduct a full AI analysis of your current resume and create a plan for improvement.
- **Assignment 2**: Rewrite and format your resume using AI tools, focusing on content and layout.
- **Assignment 3**: Tailor your resume for a specific job application using AI insights.

https://huntr.co

https://www.finalroundai.com

https://www.reejig.com/

https://aiapply.co/

https://linkedin.ideta.io

www.ingramcontent.com/pod-product-compliance
Lightning Source LLC
Chambersburg PA
CBHW050248230526
45470CB00005B/2164